THE REBEL'S BIBLE

THE REBEL'S BIBLE

DISCOVER THE STRENGTH
TO GO YOUR OWN WAY

EUGENE VASSILAS

NEW DEGREE PRESS

THE REBEL'S BIBLE

Discover the Strength to Go Your Own Way

Warning from Publisher

PLEASE NOTE: The author and publishers of this book are not and will not be held responsible, in any way whatsoever, for any improper use of the information contained within this book.

The content, stories, instructions, and advice printed in this book are not in any way intended as a substitute for medical, mental, or emotional counseling with a licensed physician or healthcare provider.

All of the following information must be used in accordance with what is permissible by law. Any damage caused as a result of the use of the content will be the exclusive responsibility of the reader or user.

It is the sole responsibility of any person planning to apply the techniques described in this book to consult a licensed physician in order to obtain complete medical information on his or her personal ability and limitations.

This is a nonfiction work. Nevertheless, names, story characteristics and other details have been modified to protect the individuals involved.

ISBN 978-1-64137-492-7 *Paperback*

978-1-64137-493-4 *Kindle Ebook*

978-1-64137-494-1 *Ebook*

Bernd Isert, this book is dedicated to you, in honor and friendship.
You showed me a new world, and then helped fill it with life.
Rest in peace.

CONTENTS

There is a time in every man's education when he arrives at the conviction that… imitation is suicide… that though the wide universe is full of good, no kernel of nourishing corn can come to him but through his toil bestowed on that plot of ground which is given to him to till. The power which resides in him is new in nature, and none but he knows what that is which he can do, nor do know until he has tried.

—RALPH WALDO EMERSON

INTRODUCTION

"Your life does not get better by chance; it gets better by change."

—JIM ROHN

One summer evening, many years ago, the front of a large truck slammed into the back of my sedan at a speed of ninety mph. The force caused my vehicle to fishtail across two lanes of highway and into the interstate divider.

In the moment before impact, my life didn't flash before my eyes. Instead, I was overcome with overwhelming grief at realizing I'd never see any of the people I loved again.

I remember thinking of my parents, then of my sister. But *I'm too young to di—* Boom! It was all over. The hood of my sedan splintered across the concrete wall, and my eyes shut for the last time.

Or so I thought.

I reopened them seconds later to realize that although my sedan was smashed, somehow—miraculously—I was not.

The accident, however, was far from over. The truck had somehow t-boned my sedan and was now pushing me sideways down the highway.

Tires squealing, engine smoking, metal shearing: it was unnatural for a car to move like this, dangling off the grille of a truck like some twisted holiday ornament. The driver, unfazed, only accelerated harder.

What is he doing? Why won't he stop? Why isn't he stopping? This didn't feel like an accident anymore.

Half a minute and some thousand meters later—our vehicles finally halted.

At this point, the driver got out and stomped in my direction: fists clenched, brows furrowed, teeth gritted, and eyes narrowed fiercely. He didn't look happy.

Where is he going? Why is he coming over here?

In my mind, it didn't make sense. After the initial collision, the driver had kept pushing my car sideways when he could have easily stopped. He didn't even brake—it's because he was trying to kill me. *Yes, that's it.* And now it looked like he was coming to finish the job.

"What did you do?!" he screamed as he reached my door. "What did you do?! Look at what you did! That's not my truck!"

I think he was insinuating that it was somehow my fault that his company vehicle was damaged.

Fuming, he grabbed around for my door handle, trying to get into my car. Thankfully, it had been smashed in. I started to worry that this guy was completely deranged.

As I screamed, "Go back to your truck!" at the top of my lungs, he started punching my car window with his bare fist.

Hard.

Again, this time even harder.

"I'm gonnna make you pay for what you diiiiid!" he slurred.

Ok, if he wasn't deranged, then he was definitely drunk.

Since I was in no condition to fight, however, my mind switched to escape strategies. *If he gets in, how do I get out? Can I get out on the passenger's side fast enough? Will that door open? Can I even move right now?*

Meanwhile, all of this was taking place in the innermost lane of the highway with cars whizzing past. Imagine I managed to get out of the car; I would still have to cross four lanes of high-speed traffic just to stand a chance of getting away.

What is the risk I get hit by another car? High.

Smoke started seeping in through the vents of the car, filling my cabin.

But what if my engine explodes with me stuck in here?

Then, as if the driver saw something off in the distance that caused a sudden change of heart, he turned around and stumbled back to his truck.

The police pulled up shortly thereafter.

PUTTING MYSELF BACK TOGETHER AGAIN

Although I spent much of the next year in the physical therapist's office tending to the pain in my neck and back, I had a whole lot to think about, too.

I felt lost and confused trying to make sense of life "after death." My family couldn't understand, my friends didn't have the tools to support me, and since I wasn't about to go therapy, I consulted no one.

Therapy, after all, was for the "weak." I wasn't weak. I couldn't be weak. No, I was strong—armored, untouchable, invincible. I was the golden boy, remember? High achiever going to a good university, running a few small businesses, popular with the ladies, etc. I didn't need help.

The result was simply that no one knew the real extent of my suffering. Even as my body started to heal and I was being told I could soon resume some normal activities, I couldn't help but think that while I didn't die in that crash, a large part of me felt like it did.

Through all this, I suffered alone. Like a typical man, I reasoned, *If I can just ignore what I'm feeling, it all might go away. If I don't think about it, it's like it never happened.*

What else could I do? Times were desperate.

THE DAY EVERYTHING CHANGED

Then, about a year later, everything changed. I got a phone call informing me that one of my best friends was in an accident and died on impact. In that instant, all the shock and fear and hopelessness from my own accident resurfaced—with a vengeance.

Attending Matt's funeral somehow felt as though I was finally attending my own. At the church, his lifeless face stared up at me from an open casket and seemed to ask, *"And what are you going to do with life now, Eugene? You got lucky with your second chance. Don't waste it."*

THE SEARCH BEGINS

I would like to tell you that the clouds parted in that moment and the answers descended on me with grace and ease. No such miracle happened.

Instead, it was more of the same for a long time: sleepless nights, endless self-questioning, anxiety, and isolation.

But slowly, in the months that followed, two things became clear. First, no one was coming to save me. If I were ever going to get out of this existential hell hole, it'd have to be through my own determination. It'd have to be me. Second, it couldn't be the *old* me. A new me would have to be born. *Old* me was gone.

In a strange way, this was fine, because *old* me had been stuck in people-pleasing and perfectionism. *Old* me had been working insane hours and was always stressed. *Old* me tried to "avoid" feeling vulnerable or insecure or hurt. In fact, *old* me was so busy pretending to be strong that he never found out what inner strength truly was. No. *Old* me was no more and a new me would have to replace him.

This revelation, as simple as it sounds, was huge for me. But it also presented a new problem. Even if I wanted to do better, I didn't know where to start or how to start. And if I didn't have the answers on how, I would need to find the teachers who did.

These teachers didn't live near me in suburban Maryland. So, I packed my bags and got ready to go to them.

REBELLION

It all seems like so long ago, but I ended up spending almost seven years traveling to fifty or so countries to live, study, and work with some of the world leaders in the human development industry.

Starting my journey, however, I was wary and scared. Many of my friends had gone off to cushy jobs on Wall Street while I was banking on finding something I couldn't yet define, in a place I'd never been, from someone I'd never met. Even if I found them, who knew if they'd be the real deal or even helpful? For a long time, it felt like my prospects for success—and sanity—were close to zero.

Then I met some promising teachers. Sure, there were lots of charlatans along the way, but these teachers were different. They were poised, wise, and their techniques worked. It soon occurred to me why I went on this journey in the first place. I was searching for *what makes man strong.*

I thought if I could just uncover the answer to that question, I might be able to feel strong again, myself. At the time, I wasn't even aware this would be the beginning of my life's work and how I'd come to serve others.

THE CHANGE BEGINS

Over the years, extended exposure to a variety of such "change specialists"—American coaches, Peruvian shamans, Indian yogis, and therapists of multiple types—changed me, too. Certain apprenticeships offered me the chance to go deeper and really see how these people lived and worked. Eventually, I took what I learned and bundled my experiences into a formula for developing inner strength. The aim? To help people cultivate the choice, courage, and confidence to go their own way.

By now, you might be wondering what exactly I learned from my teachers. For starters, I noticed they behaved more like each other than like everyone else. That is, they were a bit rebellious and they didn't take society, its problems or even people at face value. They asked provocative questions about the nature of things and developed their own opinions with the answers they received. When doing healing or helping work, they viewed both the mind and body as equally important, connected, and full of surprises.

On a personal level, I noticed they took full responsibility for their lives—even the parts that sucked. They were honest and forthright. Also, they used their time in a way that allowed them to be absurdly productive. That, and their intuitive powers were the stuff of legend.

Of course, they too had bad days. The difference was, they knew how to manage themselves in ways that got them back on track quickly. All things considered, these people gave me a map for what it means to be strong and changed my life in doing so.

HOW WE USUALLY WIND UP

To be exceptional, by definition, you have to be the exception. Unfortunately, for most people, this is where it starts to get tricky.

Most people were cornered into conformity since the time they were in diapers. Well-meaning parents, teachers, and authority figures harangued them with soul-crushing slogans like "Do as you're told," "Walk, don't run," or "Shh! Quiet down," until they finally relented.

Such incantations were supposed to teach us to "play nice" with society. On the other hand, they also established a dangerous precedent, after which, the rules and requests never ended. It turns out that adulthood has more guidelines, not fewer.

Get a well-paid job, a comfy home, a partner, then start a family, save for retirement, join a country club, etc.— ad nauseam. This is "winning at life." This is what we're "here for." To me, these goalposts, while valid, sound more like the ideas of our parents' generation and not necessarily ours.

HERE'S THE PROBLEM

Most of today's thirty-something men are stuck living brittle, one-dimensional lives.

Sure, maybe they are physically fit, but their bank account is empty. Or they've got a great job and are overweight. Or they're great parents, but their relationship is struggling. Maybe they have massive social media followings, but behind the screens, they're isolated and disconnected from themselves.

Or maybe, just maybe, in the stillness of the night, when they lay wide-eyed awake, having yet another "3 a.m. conversation" with the ceiling, the conclusion is: *despite everything I do, I still don't feel enough.*

How are we to manage? As far as coping strategies go, *distraction* seems to be very popular: eating, drinking, shopping, smoking, drugs, mechanical sex, and endless scrolling.

But there are other ways, too. For example, we often waste our time doing things we don't care about with people who don't matter to us. We go emotionally numb, so we won't have to deal with our anger or sadness, let alone our physical aches. We pretend that if we just "earn money" and "shut up," we'll be fine. We become victims of life not only evading responsibility but also evading our own strength.

But this ethos disagrees with the rebel.

INTRODUCING THE REBEL

What is a rebel, exactly?

To many, the rebel is a kind of hero because they do what is often hard and uncomfortable; they bring change when conditions are dire.

When I interviewed people and asked what they thought a rebel was, I heard everything from someone who... "challenges societal views" to "has a well-defined personal morality" to "wants to see the world burn."

From this, I concluded that a rebel is actually a multi-purpose term that doesn't refer to any one individual in isolation. You know this because you can put Mao and Mandela, Stalin and Gandhi, Che Guevara and Mother Teresa each in a sentence alongside the word rebel and you'd be understood.

To me, then, a rebel becomes an archetype or universal image of someone who goes their own way. They've cultivated choice, found courage, and built confidence in their ability to thrive. They experience more freedom and enjoyment because of it.

WHY I WROTE THIS BOOK:

I wrote this book to remind you of something you may have forgotten—that developing the inner strength to become the person you want to be is more in your reach than you might think.

Most people stop halfway on their journey. You see them around: successful business people who are fat. Fitness people who are broke. Spiritual people with poor communication skills. Rich *and* healthy people, who are living totally meaningless lives.

However, life isn't meant to be one dimensional or filled with stress, anxiety, and lack. It's meant to be lived and enjoyed in all its facets. Some might find this farfetched, if not impossible to fathom. These are people so busy surviving their one dimension, they can't even begin to think of the next.

But the truth is you don't need anything to get started. Inner strength has nothing to do with privilege, experience, or connections. All you need is the willingness to learn the skillsets that you'll find in this book and the commitment to apply them.

In the following chapters, you can expect to improve your...

- Personal autonomy: so you can become the reigning authority over your life
- Authenticity: so you feel good in your own skin and express yourself with grace and ease
- Body awareness: so you can convert this flesh-puppy into more than just an Uber for your brain
- Time awareness: so you can free yourself from the stronghold of "rushed" and make more money with less work
- Balance: in your friendships, relationships, and family dynamics
- "Surrender-ability" (whatever that means): so you can stop hustling so hard and have some more fun while creating results in your life
- ...and more!

HOW TO GET THE MOST OUT OF THIS BOOK

There is usually more than one way to get something done. That includes reading a book. Here are a few approaches for optimizing your experience with this one.

CLARIFY YOUR INTENT

Why did you pick up this book? What do you want to get from it? Think about your life, currently: do you have specific questions you want answered? If so, review the table of contents, write your questions down, and hone in on those specific chapters that might help.

With that said, know that the content within these chapters, while tested and proven, is also potentially challenging. Embracing these ideas might imply a mini-revolution in how you think, behave with others, and interact with your environment. Ironically, that is both why one reader will pick up this book and why another will put it down.

FORGET THE QUICK FIX

This may be a self-help book, but it is not a quick-fix book. Meaning, I make no claims whatsoever that the contents will magically turn a miserable life into a dream one overnight.

As I mentioned earlier, if you want real results, you must be willing to do the work. The certainty and clarity that we seek are on the other side of methodical action. With that said...

MANAGE YOUR TIME WISELY

Each chapter is an independent world of its own, so feel free to skip around. (Yes, the rebel's mindset applies here, too.)

As a philosophy teacher of mine once told me: "Even if you read a book each week for as long as you live; you won't read more than around 5,000 books. So, don't waste your time reading anything you don't like just because you're a finisher."

But just when you feel like giving up on this book, remember...

WHAT YOU MOST NEED TO FIND WILL BE WHERE YOU LEAST WANT TO LOOK

Is there a chapter title that makes you squeamish? Go there. Our aversions often point to places where we are stuck. There might be gold, in the form of learning, on the other side.

Finally, as you get started...

BE WILLING TO SUSPEND DISBELIEF

By now, you might realize this book is filled with challenging ideas. If reading these lessons challenges you half as much as learning, living, and then writing about them did me, you'll leave here tremendously enriched.

NOW MOVE, ACT... DO SOMETHING!

Remember, no rebellion ever started from the armrest of your couch.

"Why join the Navy when you can be a pirate?"

—STEVE JOBS

WHAT IS INNER STRENGTH?

"The tough-minded individual is astute and discerning. He has a strong austere quality that makes for firmness of purpose and solidness of commitment. Who doubts that this toughness is one of man's greatest needs?"

— MARTIN LUTHER KING, JR.

Abraham Lincoln once referred to himself as "the most miserable man living." He wrote, *"If what I feel were equally distributed to the whole human family, there would not be one cheerful face on the earth."* [1] Friends of his said he dripped sadness as he walked.[2]

1 "Abraham Lincoln to John Stuart, January 23, 1841." (229–230)

2 Stephen Mansfield, *Mansfield's Book of Manly Men: An Utterly Invigorating Guide to Being Your Most Masculine Self.* (188–189)

Perhaps he had good reason. As a child, he was kicked in the head by a horse. He also nearly drowned. Then, his younger brother died—followed by his mother. Lincoln had to help his father build the casket and lower her corpse into the ground. Thereafter his fiancée—the only woman he ever loved, died—followed by his sister. He suffered from malaria, smallpox, and probably syphilis.[3]

At first, things weren't much better for him professionally, either. He was rejected from law school. He failed in his first business using borrowed money. Later, he lost while running for the U.S. House of Representatives. Then he lost while running for the U.S. Senate—on two different occasions. While trying to secure his party's nomination for vice president, he lost again. Finally, however—at age fifty-one, after a lifetime of hardship—he was elected the sixteenth president of the United States. [4]

Lincoln had numerous opportunities to give up. He could have surrendered to tragedy or the thoughts of suicide that often ran through his head. But he didn't. He adapted. He persisted. He rebelled against the dark voices that came to him at night. He disciplined his mind. He became diligent in his actions. He even developed a great sense of humor.

It is true that Lincoln endured hardships few of us will ever know. And yet, this is what it took for him to become strong—strong enough to preserve the Union during the U.S. Civil

3 Chip Conley, *Emotional Equations: Simple Truths for Creating Happiness + Success* (41–42)

4 Ibid.

War, bring about the emancipation of slaves, and serve as one of the greatest presidents America has ever known.

INNER STRENGTH ISN'T ALWAYS WHAT IT SEEMS

Since the start of civilization, there have been people who stand apart from the crowd because of some special talent or skillset. Maybe they were charming politicians, visionary artists, or fierce warriors who leveraged their gifts in a way that won them favor, status, or leadership positions.

However, on a long enough timeline, it's not uncommon for such people to crack under the pressure and bend to the opinions of others. As author Robert Greene points out, these are the stories of "great senators who make lousy presidents, bold lieutenants who turn into mediocre generals or top-level managers who become incompetent executives." [5]

Then there are those who surprise us all. Even without natural talent, they rise to the occasion and go their own way. These rebels may not be organizing an uprising per se, but they still accomplish extraordinary feats of leadership and success.

How, you ask? For starters, they embrace responsibility instead of opposing it. They make hard decisions and act courageously. They leave people inspired, environments improved, and the course of history changed. What's more, most of the time, no one suspected they even had it in them.

---

5 Robert Greene, *The 50th Law.* (104–105)

These are the stories of activists Mahatma Gandhi, of naturalist Charles Darwin, and writer Fyodor Dostoyevsky—and among the rebel profiles chronicled in this book.

Keep in mind, what connects these people is not their connections or privilege or physical prowess. Many of them didn't have an education or even favorable circumstances to start. What they all had, however, was a certain quality—a fortitude, a resilience, a "grit" to endure trial by fire. In short, they had developed extraordinary amounts of inner strength. And you can too.

A WORLD OF CHALLENGE

Challenge is a part of life. On the level of basic survival, you might say, challenge *is* life: the power battles we get trapped in at work, the confused relationships that entangle our emotions, the various pulls on our time and energy.

It follows then, that how we respond to challenge largely determines the quality of our lives. Do any of the following ring true for you?

- You often feel sorry for yourself, like you can't catch a break.
- You tell yourself that you can't help the way you feel.
- You complain, procrastinate, or choose to be lazy.
- Your inner life depends on what's happening around you, not vice versa.
- You dodge the truth and deny valid criticisms.
- You go to great lengths to avoid your emotions, like sadness or embarrassment.
- You settle.

IT'S NOT YOUR FAULT

To be clear, experiencing hardship has nothing to do with you being good or bad. It's simply a fact of life. However, the problem is, most people were never shown the tools to properly handle hardship. That is, we've never learned how to become strong when we feel weak, courageous when we feel sacred, relaxed when we feel stressed, and happy when we feel sad.

Instead, we were raised on substitutes: binge-watching Netflix, chain-smoking cigarettes, and endless social media while finishing yet *another* quart of ice cream.

Substitutes may distract and delay us from the inevitable, but they never make our problems go away. What's more, people may convince themselves that by not dealing with their problems, they're staying the same, but this belief is largely false. Since life is always evolving, avoiding hardship means they're getting comparatively worse. More common than not, if your troubles go unchecked for too long, one day you wake up wedged between feelings of helplessness, hopelessness, and worthlessness, as so many of us do. This day is never a pretty one.

I say this simply now but realized it with much difficultly. For a while after my accident, I was stuck on "why me?" At the time, the victim role appeared to be a useful substitute to doing something productive to change the conditions of my life. Only later did I get to a more important question: "what now?"

I call the gap between these two questions the "hardship gap." This void is usually filled with excuses, lies, broken promises, anxiety, and stress. The wider the gap, the more problems someone must overcome. But if you ever want to taste inner strength, this is a gap that must be bridged and crossed, no exceptions.

SO, WHAT IS INNER STRENGTH?

By now you might be wondering, when I write about inner strength, what do I mean?

I certainly don't mean acting tough, hard, robotic, or numb. Inner strength, as I understand it, is an umbrella term for an aspect that touches the many dimensions of the human experience: the mental, emotional, spiritual, and even the physical.

If I were to reduce the definition of inner strength to a sentence or two, I'd say that it's the ability to resist outside pressures. At the same time, it's the ability to embrace change, especially when change is hard.

To make this kind of change easier, this book will take you through ten *actionable* principles that will help you make "heaven out of hardship," so you can find the inner strength to go your own way.

To start, let's clarify some misconceptions around what inner strength actually is—henceforth described as "strength"—for the many areas of life that it's needed:

CHAPTER 1: OWN YOUR SHIT—SELF-RESPONSIBILITY

Strength is not about pointing fingers and avoiding blame. Instead, it's pardoning your family, society, and even the weather for the conditions of your existence and taking full ownership for making your life what you want it to be—because you can.

CHAPTER 2: KEEP IT REAL—AUTHENTICITY

Strength is not about people-pleasing or living according to the group's expectations. Instead, strength is about seizing autonomy over your own life and going your own way, even when it means upsetting others.

CHAPTER 3: TRUST YOUR GUT—INTUITIONAL MASTERY

Strength is not knowing everything or needing to have all the answers. Instead, it's about nurturing your inborn (although perhaps dormant) skill of intuition. This skill will lead you to outcomes you could have never predicted, but which, in hindsight, will be better than any of those you could have devised using logic alone.

CHAPTER 4: MANAGE YOUR FEAR—CULTIVATING COURAGE

Strength is not about making fear the enemy or pretending not to be afraid. Instead, it's about learning to "befriend" fear and recruiting this emotion to help you reach your hardest goals.

CHAPTER 5: SEEK MEANING, THEN MONEY—FINDING PURPOSEFUL WORK

Strength is not about just doing something that brings in the money—and as much of it as possible while at it. Instead, your strongest and best work will be connected to something that drives meaning and purpose for you. This is important considering you will spend at least one-third of your life in this pursuit.

CHAPTER 6: STAND UP TALL—EMBODYING STRENGTH

Strength is not just washboard abs and a pumped-up body that looks good in the mirror. Instead, strength—as experienced in its physical form—translates to a body free from strain, at ease, and balanced. And whether you go to the gym or not, a strong body is much more than just an *Uber* for your brain.

CHAPTER 7: KNOW YOUR LIMITS—BUILDING PERSONAL BOUNDARIES

Strength is not about being so walled-up you can't feel or be vulnerable. Instead, it's about creating the personal boundaries that allow you to be open and connected to others, while staying strong in what you believe at the same time.

CHAPTER 8: BECOME YOUR OWN PERSON—SELF-ACCEPTANCE

Strength is not about how much love or affection you can win from others. Instead, it's about how much you can accept yourself despite your personal deficits or idiosyncrasies, and then integrate those things into who you are.

CHAPTER 9: EVOLVE BEYOND "BUSY"—OWNING TIME

Strength is not about pushing through life because you must or about you constantly doing more. Instead, learn to manage your productivity, so that it's not managing you.

CHAPTER 10: SOFTEN YOUR GRIP—LETTING GO

Strength is not about how much you can control the things in your life. Instead, it's about how much you can let go of preconceived ideas, expectations, and outcomes. The paradox of this strategy is you may not get to the exact place you thought you'd be, but you'll end up farther down the road that is right for you.

WHAT'S BEHIND INNER STRENGTH?

Inner strength is intertwined with the plight of the rebel—but also needed by anyone who's trying to live their best life.

In my personal journey and working with countless clients and groups since, I've found there to be three focus areas for building inner strength. They are *choice, courage, and confidence.*

These core areas correspond to the three parts of this book. The lessons contained within, when applied, can help any reader develop the strength to go their own way.

PART I: CHOICE

Inner strength starts as a choice. Life might have dealt you a terrible hand. Maybe you've even got a series of great excuses for why you haven't done anything about it. Ultimately, however, you have to decide if you want to stay a "victim" or become something of a "victor"—as trite as that may sound. Either way, all change starts with a choice.

PART II: COURAGE

If choice is a commitment to stretching beyond your comfort zone, then courage is the willingness to take the first step in the given direction. Ok—often it's more like a leap; this part of the process asks you to face fears, jump into the unknown, and have your limits tested throughout. However, in this stage, we begin to live beyond our perceived limits.

PART III: CONFIDENCE

If choice was what you needed to get started, and courage was what you needed to get moving, then *confidence* is what you need to keep going. Confidence is a generalized sense of "I go my own way, and it's all going to be ok" that spills out into the other areas of your life. That is, confidence keeps you progressing despite the never-ending obstacles that threaten your goals daily. As you develop in this area, life starts to present unseen realms of possibility.

THE ORIGINAL REBEL

In Greek Mythology, back when humankind was still shrouded in darkness, the Titan Prometheus stole fire from the gods and gave it to man. This original act of rebellion enabled all of civilization and human progress—but it also pissed off the gods.

In retaliation, the supreme God Zeus chained Prometheus to a rock, destining him to have his liver pecked out by hungry eagles day after day, for eternity.[6] Sorry, Prometheus.

Myths like these remind us that the things we want don't always come easily or without cost. Such is the risk we take to honor what is true within us and develop our inner strength. Not that we'll ever really know for sure, though, just from reading ideas in a book.

That's to say, cultivating inner strength is somewhat useless if it stays, well, inner. So, enjoy the stories and rebel profiles in the following chapters—but be sure to apply the skills and techniques you learn out in the world, too.

Now, let's get started.

"Life is too short to be little. Man is never so manly as when he feels deeply, acts boldly, and expresses himself with frankness and with fervor."

— BENJAMIN DISRAELI

---

6 "PROMETHEUS."

PART I

CHOICE

"You may believe that you are responsible for what you do, but not for what you think. The truth is that you are responsible for what you think, because it is only at this level that you can exercise choice. What you do comes from what you think."

— MARIANNE WILLIAMSON

It's not easy being human. But no one needs to explain that to you. You've already experienced the joys along with the woes. You've also likely felt at some point—despite everything you tried to prevent it—that another hardship was around the corner.

This is an unpopular fact of life. But most hardships—death, bankruptcy, heartbreak, or some other unwelcome change—have one good thing in common: they offer choice.

It may not seem like this at first. Most people will resist and resent hardship before they discover that what's on the other side of their unmet expectations and needs. With good reason, too: the price of change often feels too steep or the alternative too scary. It's often easier to look the other way. But hardship is simply life's way of asking: do you really, really want to go your own way?

If so, will you take responsibility for your actions instead of casting blame? Will you be yourself instead of the person you think others want you to be? Will you learn to make decisions from your gut and not be influenced by the noise of people's opinions?

These choices, by the way, are not about capability; everyone can do this if they choose. Whether we go our own way or choose to stay as we are is ultimately up to us. But the enemy is always behind the gates; we are our own main saboteurs.

Remember, if you absolutely wanted, you could leave your job today. You could ditch your failing relationship tonight. You could get on a plane and fly to South America tomorrow. You could start saving the rainforest or the refugees or even your own future right now!

The question is... what will you choose?

CHAPTER 1

OWN YOUR SHIT—SELF-RESPONSIBILITY

"A weakened sense of responsibility does not weaken the fact of responsibility."

— WILLIAM BENNETT

Once, when my sister and I were teenagers, we were driving in the car with my dad. He was huffy about something, uncentered, and had to put the car in reverse. Maybe it stalled out, maybe we were at an intersection—I don't remember, but as he put his hand behind the passenger seat, turning his body so he could look behind the car, he mistakenly dinged my sister in the side of the head. "Ow!" she yelled.

His reaction was priceless: "If your head wasn't there, I wouldn't have hit it." She darted a look at me. I looked back. We couldn't help but laugh even though we were both aghast at the implications. Not because what he said wasn't true—technically, physically speaking, it was. We were aghast because responding as he did—even if he was joking—allowed him to completely dodge responsibility.

HOW WE DODGE RESPONSIBILITY

We are all our own faults. Only when we accept this fact and take responsibility for our lives do we stop being at the mercy of the world. Until that day, however, our species has two preferred substitutes: excuses and blame. An excuse is often a reason why you can't do something. Blame, on the other hand, is an excuse pointed outwardly—at something like the government, the weather, or a pet. For example, "I didn't have time" is an excuse but "my partner made me late" is a form of blame. Both devices are nefarious, subtle, and widely used. Do any of the following ring true for you?

- You find it uncomfortable to sit with the fact that you did something wrong.
- You often complain about what's wrong in your life.
- You hold lengthy grudges when someone offends or hurts you.
- You resent people for what they have if you don't have equal or better.
- You suffer in a way other people could never understand.
- You tend to use absolute statements ("You always do X to me!).
- You think life is unfair, so *why not* blame someone else?

WHY WE DON'T WANT TO BE RESPONSIBLE

We spend the first nine months of our lives floating in a full-service, all-inclusive, uterine spa. It's climate-controlled, stocked with food, and rent-free. Then, once we exit the womb, we continue relying on our caretakers for everything from protection to food to love. Our dependent status only shifts as we grow from children into adults and learn how to be responsible for ourselves in this strange, messy world.

But the journey from dependent to dependable isn't easy. Furthermore, initiating this process rips us from the safety and comfort of childhood. We are therefore required to evolve our personalities and enter a new era of unknowns. To foreswear or delay this task is to cripple our potential for inner strength as adults.

The problem is very few people willingly give up their habits and comfortable ways. That's why societies have historically ushered people into adulthood with a ceremony or rite of passage: i.e. *baptism, bar mitzvah,* or *quinceañera* among others. These rituals helped publicly announce that the child had now been reborn as an adult—and would henceforth be held to the hallmark of adulthood: responsibility.

Of course, there are those of us who simply won't grow up. As adults, these people are stuck in regressive cycles and find themselves taking drugs to feel good, holding jobs that barely pay rent, and overusing technology to avoid the conditions of their life. These people suffer greatly. What's more, they also often point their suffering outward in the form of blame.

BLAME HAS INFECTED OUR LIVES

We live in a culture of blame: It has contaminated our legal system, work cultures, and private lives.

For example, each year, billions of dollars trade hands in legal proceedings because someone's coffee was too hot, dog was badly trained, or high doorstep was unmarked. Meanwhile, at the office, our boss preaches collaboration and support, but as soon as their neck is on the line, they remind us how it's really every employee for themselves.

We bring blame home, too. If our partners don't meet our needs, we're often quick to frame their behaviors as mean or bad. This gives us the "right" to get offended and wave the blame finger, as opposed to looking for our own responsibility in managing the crying kid, filling the empty fridge, or paying overdue bills.

Overall, this is not the worst news. The worst news is this: our culture of blame is unlikely to change because blame is practically built into the human experience through language.

For example, did you ever notice how the English sentence "Sam made me angry" is accepted and grammatical, but the equivalent, "I did anger in my body when Sam said that" is not? The second one is probably more accurate, but it also sounds weird. So, let's just blame that patsy, Sam, and be done with it, shall we?

GETTING WEASELLY WITH OUR WORDS

Working with a variety of coaching clients over the years, I've noticed a widespread tendency for people to use "weasel phrases"—as I like to call them. Weasel phrases are ennobling sentences. They assert our innocence and excuse us from taking responsibility for the conditions of our lives.

For example, have you, or someone you've known, ever said:

- "That's just the way things are." (Translation: I don't care to look for alternatives.)
- "I had no choice; I did what I had to do." (Translation: my capacity for creative thought is minimal.)
- "I'm just that type of person." (Translation: I'm stuck in this role or persona.)
- "Sorry, I'm just following orders. It's out of my hands." (Translation: I like to little spoon with authority.)
- "It doesn't matter what I do, nothing will change anyway." (Translation: I'm a fortune-teller; want me to predict your future, too?)
- "They made me do it." (Translation: I'm a groupie...or puppet...or both.)

To be clear, the words themselves are not the problem. Rather, what's problematic is how we artfully assemble these words to weasel out of doing the thing we don't want to do.

THE PROBLEM WITH NOT TAKING RESPONSIBILITY

We generally don't take responsibility when doing so somehow feels uncomfortable or dangerous. My question for you is: what if it were more dangerous not to be accountable for your actions?

I had to think about this a lot as a childhood asthmatic. For example, once, while out walking with my parents as a child, I had an unexpected asthma attack. Mom didn't bring my inhaler. Dad didn't either. Looking back, why would they? I was the one with the respiratory disease; it was—and had been, for years—my responsibility to carry my aerosol lifeline.

Still, as my trachea tightened to the width of a red coffee stirrer, I wheezed blame at them. "You… should... have... brought... the... Ventolin!"

This effort, strangely enough, did nothing to promote airflow; it may have even restricted my breathing further.

My parents were too busy taking me to the emergency room to dignify my accusations. While very understanding and loving about what transpired, they didn't buy into my blame game for a second.

"Your lungs, your life," they told me.

And so it was—and has been—ever since.

TAKING RESPONSIBILITY WILL MAKE YOU STRONGER

Responsibility is not innate—it's a skill. This skill must be learned and practiced regularly. It's also one of the most important prerequisites to developing inner strength.

Rebels somehow understand this almost intuitively. They see responsibility having two parts: "response" and "ability" or *the ability to respond.* To them, responding implies choice. It comes from a place of awareness. Responding promotes freedom.

On the other hand, most people don't do "response-ability" as much as they do "react-ability," which explains the blame pandemic. Reaction, unfortunately, is mechanical. It's unconscious and enslaving. Worst of all, it's based on something old—some disempowered situation of the past—that is then repeated in the present. By contrast, rebels are concerned about defining something new. Their objective is more choice, more awareness, and more strength in the present and future.

The late writer, Stan Lee, once said: "With great power comes great responsibility." For our purposes, the inverse is also true: With great responsibility comes great power. Here's how you can get a bit more of both in your life today.

OWNING YOUR SHIT WILL MAKE YOU STRONGER

REBEL TIPS FOR RESPONSIBILITY

Start By Becoming Responsible To Yourself

Taking responsibility for the conditions of life is harder to do when you're hungry, tired, and can't remember where you left your keys. So, make sure your nutrition, sleep, hygiene, and organizational needs are sorted and that you're not walking around deficient in the basics. Being responsible to others is a natural outgrowth of being responsible for yourself first.

Acknowledge the price you're already paying

Every decision you make has its obligatory price. You don't get to choose whether you pay or not; you only get to choose which one you pay for. For example, do you prefer to pay the price of being responsible—as in admitting fault, keeping promises, and becoming dependable—even if it requires months, years, or even a lifetime of uncomfortable self-examination? Or do you prefer to pay the price of blaming and excusing—namely more crippling self-enslavement and illusion? The choice is yours.

Build the Skills

Decide what you can influence in each situation versus what you can't. If you can influence something but don't yet have the result you're hoping for, ask yourself: what skills would I need to develop in order to get this result? For example, I was bullied when I was a kid. A subsequent martial arts teacher of mine told me if a bully is throwing punches, you can either keep getting beat up and blame the bully, or you can learn to block.

Become solution-focused

All justifications, frustration, resistance, blame, and excuses are placeholders for actually finding a better solution. If you can't take responsibility for the situation as it is, try accepting responsibility for finding a new solution to the problem.

Mind your tongue

Commit to a new standard of "word hygiene." Get concrete in your language: no more wishing, hoping, trying. Strike the words "might" and "maybe" from your lexicon. Then, listen for instances where you bend language so you can skirt responsibility:

For example:

- Are you late because there was traffic—or because you didn't leave the house on time?
- Are you "too busy" to pursue your dream job—or is it just not a priority?
- Did the plant die because of the "flaky, bad soil"—or because you forgot to water it?
- Is your job overly stressful—or do you not prioritize time for evening relaxation?
- And perhaps most importantly, did the donut *really* make you eat it?

Flex your Empathy muscle

Blame bars you from feeling empathy for others. It dehumanizes you. That's not to say you're responsible for the feelings of others, but you are responsible for your own behavior. Consider the situations in which you make excuses or blame. How might this habit be subtly impacting other people?

REBEL CASE STUDY:

Kyle Maynard has no hands. He has no feet. His arms end at his elbows. His legs end at his knees. And yet he's climbed Mount Kilimanjaro, been a nationally-ranked wrestler, and speaks on stages all over the world.

Maynard was born in 1986 with a genetic deformity called congenital amputation. His parents—ruling out the possibility of an abortion before he was born—chose not to treat Maynard any differently once he came into the world, either.[7]

It might have been understandable for Maynard to stay dependent all his life. After all, he couldn't walk, stand, or eat on his own. But at some point, his father, as a way of prompting Maynard to take more responsibility for himself, announced that he would stop feeding the boy. That is, his son would have to learn to feed himself.

This might seem harsh, but the challenge provoked in Maynard an idea: that despite his handicap, if he dutifully applied himself, he could still make things happen— his way.

Implementation, however, was harder than expected. Maynard dropped his spoon thousands of times while learning to eat. He failed at putting on his own socks until the age of fifteen. Showering, brushing his teeth, and typing never

7 Bryn Swartz, "Heart of A Champion: The Unbelievable Story of Kyle Maynard."

became "ordinary" tasks for him. Then, when he got into athletics, he lost thirty-five middle school wrestling matches in a row.

Still, he persisted. He worked with a coach and got feedback on his technique. He modified his approach until he finished his high school career with thirty-five victories and only sixteen losses. He went on to win athletic awards and write a book about his life.

"No obstacle would keep me from accomplishing my dreams…I didn't quit or give up. I met the adversity with a full head of steam," Maynard said.[8]

It seems since the day his dad put down the spoon—or arguably earlier—Maynard was faced with a choice: disability or responsibility. While his conditions are certainly unique, his choice is not unlike the choice we must make every day for ourselves.

"Each man is questioned by life. He can only answer to life by answering for his own life; he can only respond by being responsible."

— VIKTOR E. FRANKL, PSYCHIATRIST, HOLOCAUST SURVIVOR, AND AUTHOR OF MAN'S SEARCH FOR MEANING

8 "Kyle Maynard Makes No Excuses."

CHAPTER 2

KEEP IT REAL—AUTHENTICITY

"Be yourself; everyone else is already taken."

— OSCAR WILDE

Paulo had a lot going for him: business savvy, razor wit, Hollywood looks, and the build of a young Schwarzenegger. Interesting and humorous tidbits practically spilled out of his mouth the day we met. He seemed like a cool guy, so the next time I went to a group dinner with other entrepreneurs, I invited him along. We caught up in the car on the way, trading business ideas and world views.

However, the moment we stepped into the house where the gathering was being held, something shifted. It was as though Paulo became someone else—like he stepped into a role of some sort. He began to speak obnoxiously loudly, as if he wanted everyone at the event to hear him. Then, when we were seated at the dinner table and the host was speaking, Paulo made a point to interrupt—repeatedly—with stuff that didn't make sense.

What got giggles from the group at first soon received coughs and a few glares. What's more, Paulo's narrative seemed to always insinuate how good and smart and successful he was. In other words, the gravitas I experienced from him in an individual setting seemed absent in the presence of the group. But where did it go?

On the way home, I gently broached the topic with Paulo. He confessed there was a split between who he wanted people to think he was and who he felt himself to be. Basically, people saw him as Hercules, but he really felt closer to Ronald McDonald.

I, too, knew the authenticity battle well from my own upbringing. I told him, were he interested, that I could help. A few days later, he signed up to work with me; what follows is some of what I taught him.

THE PROBLEM WITH SELF-IMAGE

Each one of us has an inner picture in our imagination of how we see ourselves. This self-image is basically an inner map from which our behavior generates. If we don't like the inner picture, we'll often build a pretend one. None of this usually happens consciously, of course. When I asked Paulo about his self-image, he said, "I feel like a little boy in this big man's body."

His solution had been to build a compensatory "big man identity." This version of himself was loud, "fun," and always the center of attention. Anytime Paulo was uncomfortable, he brought out the *big man*. This is what he did when we walked into the house, leaving his *inner boy* to wait in the safety of the car until we finished dinner and drove home.

KILLERS OF AUTHENTICITY

Comedian Chris Rock once said, "When you meet somebody for the first time, you're not meeting them, you're meeting their representative." The representative he's referring to is also known as a *persona*: a pretend or augmented version of you. Often, it's the "you" that you wish you were minus any of your negative traits (*persona* literally means "mask" in Latin). The persona helps hide the "you" you're afraid you might actually be.

Your persona shows up in many ways in place of a strong, integrated self. Do any of the following ring true for you?

- You need people to like and praise you... often.
- You don't tell others when you're mad or offended.
- You're happy to talk about your accomplishments but not your shortcomings.
- You think you can control what people think about you.
- You think it's your job to manage how people around you feel.
- You don't feel relaxed sharing or admitting mistakes.
- You're often caught in big groups even though you're actually an introvert.

- You secretly feel *wrong* not only in your behavior but as a person.

IS THIS OUR FAULT?

Humans are not meant to live alone. We're wired to live in groups, and the setup of our brains is social.[9] Apparently, this is true to the extent that if we're excluded from the group, we feel distress in the same brain areas that process physical pain.[10]

What this means is that we're always seeking balance between *us* and *them*. If we align too much with other people, the risk is we lose ourselves. If we align too much with ourselves, we could easily be branded sociopaths or even get kicked out of the group.

This may not seem like a big deal now, but for our ancestors, tribal exclusion often meant death. At a minimum, it implied a loss of protection, food, and housing options. Mating probably became a long shot, too. Suffice it to say, there was a lot at risk. Maybe that's why today we're still willing to "fake it" until we make it.

---

9 Wendy Palmer and Susan Crawford. Leadership Embodiment: *How the Way We Sit and Stand Can Change the Way We Think and Speak.* (141)

10 Naomi Eisenberger, et al, "An Experimental Study of Shared Sensitivity to Physical Pain and Social Rejection."

THE TENDENCY STARTS EARLY

We usually start to "fake it"—that is, build our personas—in childhood, as an act of self-protection.

Frank Pucelik, the Co-Founder of NLP and a mentor of mine, described such a childhood. He grew up with alcoholic parents who fought a few nights a week until one of them was unconscious, bloody, or both.

"I expected to come out of my bedroom some mornings and find one or both of them dead," he said. "My dad didn't exist and my mother... she was physically dangerous... so I got beat up a lot as a kid. I could never figure out what the hell I did that was so bad, that I deserved to be raised in the house with that much chaos and that much physical violence all the time... I hated it so much that it must have been my fault. My fault—you know—kids get those ideas sometimes," he said.

Pucelik's story points to how hurt people often hurt others unless reformed. Kids raised by troubled adults—who act unpredictably and tend to withdraw love often—end up troubled themselves. This could describe much of Pucelik's early adulthood. But after he went to Vietnam to serve in the war, something slowly started to change.

"After all my time with my parents being drunks, after so much energy that I had in me from the jungle... I'm afraid I wasn't a very nice guy for years... but I understood that this is not going to work; I'm going to be in prison, or I'm going to be dead or both. And this is not who I want to be."

It was only at that point that Pucelik decided to lift the mask and do the work to heal himself. Since then, he has committed his life to helping others do the same.

THE RISK OF INAUTHENTICITY

Back to Paulo, who we met earlier in the chapter. As we rode home from the event that night, he confessed how much he was suffering across the different areas of his life. Sure, social scenarios triggered him in such a way that he reverted to his people-pleasing, *big man* identity. But his private relationships were no better. He claimed to have a habit of attracting manipulative personalities. They would tell him what he wanted to hear and then get him to do favors for them. The result was that he constantly felt angry and even "used." He wouldn't confront them openly, however. Instead, he would emotionally withdraw or start to "phase them out," as he put it. This pattern would repeat every one to three months or so. At that point, a relationship with someone new would rise from the ashes of the old one.

His reasoning: "I think women only like me for my body."

Mine: "You're probably right."

Pause.

"Wait, what?" he questioned.

"If you're not sharing who you really are with them, what else could they like?" I said.

"Well, they can't handle the real me, that's for sure," he said.

"What do you mean? What's the real you? Have I met him? Can you handle the *real* you?"

"The real me is bad, man."

"Bad or badass?"

"No, bad… as in evil."

"*Evil* Paulo? I like the sound of that. Tell me more. What's so bad about him?"

"Sometimes I feel like a crazy person. I say and do stuff that's not normal. I pretend to be 'Mr. Nice Guy' until I get so bitter and resentful, I can't stand it anymore. Then I lash out and scream at everyone in my way. Or if I don't scream, I'll act like a bully and be mean and really critical. It's like I don't care. I just have to get the pain out. It doesn't matter who is in my way. I tell myself I can do that because at the end of the day, I don't need anyone. I don't *need* friends, so it doesn't matter what I do."

"Oh. So, you're just describing your inner beast."

"Yes. My inner beast is fucking evil!"

By *inner beast*, I was affectionately referring to the part of his self-image that he rejects as negative. The "shadow self." His "inner monster." His Mr. Hyde. The *inner beast*. We've all got one.

Getting to know this inner part, I've found, is one of the most important things we can do in our pursuit of a more authentic life. Ask yourself: what has to happen for the beast to come out? When it does, what does it want? And what calms the beast down?

By acknowledging your inner beast, you stop being possessed by it. You interface voluntarily, not accidentally. Then, as you build a relationship with this part and make it feel included in your life, your other personas fade. That is, you no longer have a need for a "representative." What's more, few people can attack you, because you've inventoried and accounted for what you formerly tried to hide: fears, insecurities, weaknesses, foibles, perversions, doubts, and traumas. This may all sound weird, but it works.

In general, accepting your capacity for both good and evil reduces your need to convince anyone that you're anything but yourself. That's when your persona gets to permanently retire.

BEING YOURSELF WILL MAKE YOU STRONGER

REBEL TIPS FOR AUTHENTICITY

GET TO KNOW YOUR MOST COMMON PERSONA(S)

We all want to be liked and accepted. What do you do when there's a risk that you won't be? What personas do you employ? What are they like? Take a moment to write them down. In what situations do they appear? In the above example, Paulo had to be around groups of successful business people in order to enact this persona. On the other hand, he didn't really bring his persona out with me.

Sometimes it's Good to be Bad

Your inner beast has a purpose. Remember, the world is filled with people whose interests are unaligned with your own. Such people are often happy to use aggression, manipulation, and deception to achieve their wants and needs. But if you can't recognize and appreciate this capacity in yourself, how could you effectively manage it when it comes from others? Your beast helps you defend against the plots that prevent you from going your own way.

Hire an interim CEO for your mind

Some people tend to defer to other people's decisions or perspectives before considering their own. If that's you, start reversing that order. Consult with others only after you've made your own decision on the matter at hand, no matter how tentative it may be.

For example, imagine there was such a thing as an Inner CEO... and you hired one. This new "part" of you knows what to do, how to do it, and always has the final say. With this Inner CEO in charge, if someone asked you how you knew you did a good job on something, you'd respond "because I felt good about it" as opposed to "I could see other people had a positive reaction" or "someone told me that I did a good job."

The point is that henceforth, on all matters pertaining to the self, your imaginary Inner CEO gets to make the final call. You can always go back to petitioning the tribe later.

Be Patient as you Come Undone

The hardest thing about living more authentically is the process of coming undone—an uncertain process that happens in small bumps and bursts and excites no one. It may take time to release your persona and finally feel at peace with who you are—but if you do the inner work, it will happen.

Celebrate your uniqueness

In his books *Callings* and *Vital Signs*, author Gregg Levoy catalogs the wavering process of discovering who you are and what life holds for you. Then, in our interview together, he reiterated the importance of celebrating your personal uniqueness. Speaking of his own life, he said:

"For one thing, I'm a twin. So that's like three percent of the population, literally 33 out of 1,000 births. I'm a lefty—that's one out of ten. I'm self-employed—that's another one out of ten. Oh, I'm an artist—that's 1.4% of the total American workforce. And then, like you, I'm devoted to the inner life: I don't know how many people do that on a regular basis. I've also moved twenty-three times in fifteen years. So, I'm more of a nomad than I'm a settler. You know, I identify as a rebel, in the sense of someone who doesn't follow the script. And there's something kind of empowering about that."

To put it in my own words: find what's unique about you and keep celebrating this fact until the roots of strength begin to burrow into your heart, mind, and soul.

"Only the truth of who you are, if realized, will set you free."

— ECKHART TOLLE

REBEL CASE STUDY:

Wolfgang Amadeus Mozart started playing the piano in 1760. He was four years old. Wolfgang's father, Leopold—himself a composer, teacher, and player of the piano—noticed his son's promise and pushed young Wolfgang to improve.

Strangely enough, the boy loved to practice on his own and had to be dragged away from the piano each night. Soon Leopold decided to bring his son to play in the capital cities of Europe.

Royal audiences lauded the little prodigy. During his performances, Wolfgang displayed incredible talent and improvised elaborate melodies. His performances started to generate something of a reputation for him among the high courts, as well as a comfortable income for the family.

As Wolfgang grew in age and recognition, however, things changed. He still loved the piano but discovered his knack and preference for composing. A deep struggle ensued for Wolfgang: on one hand, he wanted to satisfy his father, who demanded his son perform the conservative music that would please the courts and keep paying the family's bills. On the other hand, Mozart wanted to honor his own creative vision and not be artistically stifled.

If he did the former, he felt as though he would be dishonoring himself. If he did the latter, he feared he'd be dishonoring his father—something the overbearing, patriarchal Leopold would find intolerable.

As a way of coping, Mozart developed something of a 'good boy' persona. That is, instead of following his heart, he became a 'dutiful, obedient child'—even into adulthood. What this meant was that the prodigy stopped speaking of his dreams and desires and instead started complaining about the conditions of his life—the conditions he felt he could not change.

Several stifling years passed like this for Wolfgang in Salzburg. At some point, however, he had enough and approached his father with a proposition to leave the country and go to France. A compromise was reached: Wolfgang could go live in Paris, but he would need to work as a conductor and continue supporting the family.

In retrospect, this compromise satisfied no one. Wolfgang went to Paris, but when he got there, he didn't like the city and found the job stifling. Moreover, his mother, who had accompanied him on the journey, got sick and died on her return home to Austria.[11]

Later, when Wolfgang went back to Salzburg, he did so with a bowed head. He found work as a court organist, and the nightmarish job stirred within him a deep resentment of self and others. Each day, he wrestled with the implications of continuing to live under the reign of his father, versus becoming his own person.

---

11 Stanley Sadie, "Wolfgang Amadeus Mozart."

At some point, he decided to make his complaints known to his father. "I am a composer... I neither can nor ought to bury the talent for composition with which God in his goodness has so richly endowed me." [12]

Leopold, sensing Wolfgang's defiance, reminded him of how much the boy had been given. Leopold not only grew angry but also jealous and eventually tried to stifle his son's career in an effort to keep Wolfgang in line.

In 1781, Wolfgang rebelled, leaving for Vienna and vowing never to return to Salzburg. His father never forgave him for abandoning the family. [13]

Wolfgang's decision to leave, and his father's reaction, caused a family rift that would never be healed. Once he left, however, Wolfgang composed his most famous operas and in doing so, changed the world of music forever. This is something he could have never done pretending to be someone he was not.

---

12 Robert Greene, *Mastery.* (52–54)

13 Ibid.

CHAPTER 3

TRUST YOUR GUT—INTUITIONAL MASTERY

"The intuitive mind is a sacred gift and the rational mind is a faithful servant. We have created a society that honors the servant and has forgotten the gift."

— ALBERT EINSTEIN

Years ago, I left a nightclub at 2 a.m. with a pounding headache. Out front was a row of taxis, but I chose to walk home instead, thinking it would clear my head. I had just moved to Buenos Aires and was young, directionless, and brash, all at once.

I'll figure it out on the way, I told myself. Twenty minutes later, when I actually managed to find the street on which I lived, for some reason the street dead-ended in train tracks and not my apartment complex.

No problemo for Eugenio. Because folded in my pocket was a big paper map of Palermo—supposedly the trendiest, safest neighborhood in all of Argentina.

While reviewing my map under a streetlight, I realized that I wasn't in Palermo anymore. Plus, I was on the wrong side of the train tracks. It looked like I had no choice but to go back to the club and take a taxi from out front.

When I looked up from the map, however, I noticed someone in the distance. It struck me as a bit odd that someone would be standing in the middle of the sidewalk at 2 a.m. Were they also lost? Were they watching me? They weren't there before. This seemed strange.

Don't jump to conclusions. Just because you're in an unfamiliar country, walking down a dark street, and there's a person standing nearby in the shadows doesn't mean anything. Maybe that's just what Argentines do—hang out and people watch at 2 a.m.

I shoved my map in my pocket and started walking back from where I came, which led me closer to the unidentified person. In retrospect, I realize I could have crossed to the other side of the street, but I didn't. I was used to ignoring inner signals back then. So, true to habit, I just kept walking closer toward the person. And they didn't move.

Twenty-five feet.

Fifteen feet.

When I got within ten feet I realized that the person was a man and that his eyes were piercing through the darkness and set on me. At that point, my brain stopped playing Marco Polo with reality and caught up to the unfolding moment.

In under a second, my stomach started churning. My palms got cold and sweaty. My mouth went dry and my throat tightened. My heart pounded beneath my coat. My eyes shifted between the figure ahead and possible escape routes. I looked to my left, then right; there was no room left to run. I was too late.

Unsurprisingly, the figure lurched toward me. I pushed him back and tried to dash, but then suddenly two others jumped out of the darkness to join in on the fun.

Me against three? I don't know how to defend myself against a group. A barrage of fists met my face and body from all sides. My head jerked back. I went into a daze.

Luckily for me, they wanted money more than spilled blood. This became clear as they ran through my coat pockets while I ducked oncoming punches with lessening resolve.

A few random nickels fell out of my coat pocket and onto the sidewalk. It probably seemed like they were robbing Oliver Twist.

"*Este hijo de puta no tiene nada.*" (This lovely gentleman doesn't have anything).

Eventually, I broke free and bolted home with two black eyes and a life lesson about listening to my intuition.

WHY WE HAVE INTUITION

Wild birds still use it to find their nests halfway around the globe. Deer and other prey use it to not get eaten in the forest. Firefighters use it to find and free trapped people in burning buildings. Security guards use it to reduce theft at a department store. Doctors use it to identify and cure illnesses. Intuition is all around us. And it starts inside.

The word intuition is derived from the Latin *intueri*, which means "to see within, to contemplate or to look upon."

Your intuition, then, is a sort of inner intelligence and early warning system that comes factory-installed and works below the level of consciousness to keep you thriving. It allows you to process the eleven million bits of information absorbed from your senses quickly and subliminally.[14] That's really important and useful because if decision-making was left strictly to our conscious minds, our processing capacity would be limited to under fifty bits per second. Translation: We. Wouldn't. Be. Able. To. Complete. A sentence. Without. Getting. Overwhelmed. Not to mention big choices, like selecting a mate, or a new job, or a home would become nearly impossible because of their complexity. Simply put, humanity would not progress without intuition.

---

14 George Markowsky, "Physiology."

WE'VE TUNED OUT OUR INTUITION

Isn't it interesting that most of us are more likely to take the advice of the drunk person sitting next to us at the bar rather than listen to our gut? Why? Perhaps because intuition, by definition, is not rational. You can't measure it, you can barely control it, so how could you trust it? Not to mention, it just sounds weird. It's akin to "feeling," "sensing," and "dreaming." It's something too ethereal and *feminine* for most men—and more fit for the witches, mysticism, and superstition of the Middle Ages, as author Gregg Levoy points out.[15]

Some of us have even had bad experiences with intuition and shut it away forever. For example, that time you found a dress shirt in your laundry that wasn't yours—and it certainly didn't belong to your partner of four years—and your *intuition* screamed *affair.* However, when you brought it up, your partner angrily reminded you it was actually your brother's and that you were now sleeping on the couch until further notice. Remember that?

Others go as far as to call intuition unscientific or even misleading. For example, no amount of intuition will get me to land a jumbo jet if I've never been to flight school or sat in a plane's cockpit (despite what the movies suggest). Or, as another example, there are millions of stockbrokers earning average returns—or even losing money—despite their *intuitive* stock picking.

---

15 Gregg Levoy, *Callings: Finding and Following an Authentic Life* (20–22)

EVERYDAY INTUITION

Intuition may have earned itself a bad rep over the millennia, but without it, many parts of our lives begin to suffer. Do any of the following ring true for you?

- You sometimes get hunches, but you don't pay them much attention because you can't explain them.
- You often say to yourself, "I'll never do that again," only to catch yourself repeating the act.
- You hit the same or similar block each time you attempt to reach a goal.
- You get into sub-optimal relationships too quickly or stay in them too long.
- You avoid risk even if the people around you would consider it "healthy."
- You experience life as a never-ending hustle, ignoring subtle signs when it's time to transition.
- You dismiss out-of-the-box ideas as fleeting distractions.

NOT JUST MORE INTUITION, BETTER INTUITION

We all can access intuition. The dilemma, however, is that intuition is a skill. It needs to be cultivated and tested against reality. Intuition serves your highest good when you have information and experience in a certain domain and can quickly discern patterns or similarities. That's what informs your gut reaction or "hunch": the fact that at some point in your life, you've seen this deck of cards already. Over time, that's what helps us develop a similar, near instinctive processing speed—the human version of having the ears of a wolf, the eyes of an owl, or reflexes of a jaguar.

On the other hand, if you blindly follow your feelings or listen to your ego, you might end up walking home early one morning in a city you do not know and turning into a dark alley for a fist massage. Please, for the sake of my younger self, learn to discern what is intuition and what is just twenty-something bravado.

The good news is that the longer we are alive, the vaster our repertoires of experience become. It's the same reason why chess masters use mental decision trees for their next move (i.e. *if I move my piece there, I can attack, or over there, I can defend*) but later evolve to a type of processing in which they quickly and intuitively simulate various outcomes—leaving only the highest and best next move.[16]

When you and I apply intuition to other parts of our lives, we are doing roughly the same thing. Here are a few steps for living your life more intuitively.

TRUSTING YOUR GUT WILL MAKE YOU STRONGER

REBEL TIPS FOR INTUITION

GET QUIET

Make the practice of being alone a more regular one, even if only for a few minutes per day. That way, you can start to separate the outer noise from your inner "still, small voice," as Gandhi called it. Hand-held technologies are not invited

---

16 Gary A. Klein, *The Power Of Intuition: How Do Use Your Gut Feelings To Make Better Decisions At Work.* (107)

to your sanctuary of silence, wherever and whenever that may be.

Stop waiting for lightning bolts & thunderclaps

Life rarely communicates with us through loud, perfectly timed lightning bursts and thunderclaps. If this happens, it's usually too late. Instead, look for subtleties. For example, maybe you get the intuition to call someone you haven't talked to in years, and they're tragically dying of cancer. Maybe you read the inside cover of a book that was deserted on the coffee shop table, and you get a new insight on how to solve a problem in your life. Clues to our questions come wrapped in many disguises.

Do your homework, then let go

When making a decision, you might start by gathering information, analyzing risk, and then evaluating your options. Following that, after enough research, your best move might be an intuitional one. Even scientists admit that it's the following of their intuition that leads to new discoveries, much like a dog follows a scent with its nose to find a buried bone. With practice, you'll even get comfortable making everyday decisions with intuition and then moving to analysis if more follow-up is needed.

Implement milestones

Having said that, when facing a risky undertaking, you may want to let your intuition lead but also establish a baseline metric against which to measure your progress. For example, it takes roughly two months to climb Mount Everest. If you find you're already halfway through your allotted food after only a week into the climb, knowing your daily food consumption milestone will help you adjust your operation and survive. Then you can be intuitional about whether you proceed upward or head back to basecamp.

Learn to Discern

Intuition can also help you live a more discerning, aligned life. Doing so, however, will require that you consistently stress-test your theories of life. Are they true? How do you know? Are they based on sufficient experience and training? If not, look around. Notice stuff. Test things out. Record the results. Learn from your mistakes. Repeat.

Become a Whole-Body Listener

Your body is always informing your intuition and vice versa. Just observe someone's body language: notice how they cross their arms, shrug their shoulders, or furrow their eyebrows in relation to what you say. Try observing your own inner landscape, too. Does your stomach tighten every time you have to talk to your boss? Do certain muscles twitch when you walk down a dark alley? Do you get a weird headache every time you call your mother?

Nature sound recorder Gordon Hampton was once in the woods capturing sounds when a fit of anxiety overtook him. He ditched his equipment as it was still recording and took off running. When he came back and replayed the track, he heard the growl of a leopard. "I was being a whole-body listener, and my rational mind was trying to fight it." [17]

Trust yourself

Remember, intuition is not a guarantee, it's a gamble.[18] You can't *will* an intuition into happening, but when it does, ask: *how does this fit my previous experience? Have I experienced something similar in the past?* It might take some time until your raw impulses are interpreted as useful, but with practice, your intuition will evolve into a reliable skill you can trust.

> *"Dull minds are never either intuitive or mathematical."*
>
> — BLAISE PASCAL

---

17 Greg Levoy, *Callings.*

18 Garth Sundem, *Beyond IQ.* (89)

REBEL CASE STUDY:

When Charles Darwin was just a boy, he could spend hours outside, hunting, collecting flowers, observing insects and birds in their native habitat. His father—a wealthy doctor, who wanted his son to be "traditionally" successful—dismissed this behavior as part of a flailing hobby, at best. He had other aspirations for young Charles.[19]

But in grade school, Charles didn't excel in Latin or Greek and was mediocre in Algebra. Desperate to make something of the boy, his father shipped him off to medical school. But Charles couldn't handle blood either and subsequently dropped out. The whole time, in the back of his mind, he fought his father's criticisms: "You care for nothing but shooting, dogs, and rat-catching, and you will be a disgrace to yourself and all your family." What if his father was somehow right? [20]

Charles soon got enrolled in Cambridge University by the grace of his father's connections. By 1831, with intense effort, Charles earned a bachelor's degree. It was then that something unexpected happened: a former professor forwarded Charles an invitation. It was for an unpaid, multi-year internship aboard the ship *HMS Beagle.* The position? A naturalist. Charles's task would be to collect plant and mineral

19 Robert Greene, *Mastery.* (26–30)

20 Ibid.

specimens from around the globe and bring them back to England for examination.

When he consulted his father about this opportunity, he was barred from going. His father claimed that such a trip would derail him from his career path. It looked like Charles had no choice but to decline the invitation. But his gut persisted. It wouldn't let up. Charles couldn't explain why but felt he'd be making a mistake if he didn't go. So, against his father's counsel, Charles went back and accepted the offer. A few months later, he set sail aboard *The Beagle.*

At once, Charles regretted his decision. The first weeks on the journey were stomach-wrenching and spent in the company of sea-faring lunatics, namely Captain FitzRoy and his crew. Moreover, Charles was constantly seasick and felt like an idiot for disobeying his father. His intuition must have been wrong.

But once *The Beagle* arrived at the shores of Brazil, Charles understood why he had taken the intuitive leap: he had reached a naturalist's haven.

He caught and captured birds, crabs, spiders, and butterflies never before seen in England.

Later, when *The Beagle* sailed to Argentina and Charles continued exploring, he found fossil remains fused in the cliffs—bones and horse-like teeth that seemed to point to an unidentified species that no longer existed. The same was true about seashell fossils he found while hiking the Andes mountains, some 12,000 feet above sea level. How did they get up there, he wondered?

It was soon 1835, and *The Beagle* arrived on the shores of the Galapagos islands. There, Charles noticed unique species of lizards, tortoises, fish, snakes, and insects that he hadn't ever seen before, even on other islands fifty miles away. He deduced that each island had totally unique species—each with special markings and beaks. These findings seemed to suggest that life had evolved differently in these isolated places over time. That is, not according to some Divine plan but rather to some evolutionary pattern.

With this finding and after nearly five years at sea, *The Beagle* returned to the shores of England, where Charles and his father reunited. The boy Mr. Darwin once knew was gone. In his stead stood a man, whose eyes were fierce with purpose and whose head was filled with the ideas that would soon form the famous *Theory of Biological Evolution.*

By heeding his intuition, Charles ultimately stumbled on his life's work and changed the very way we conceive of science, humanity, and life itself.

PART II

COURAGE

"You cannot cross a chasm in two small jumps."

—DAVID LLOYD GEORGE, BRITISH STATESMAN.

If choice brings us to the point of no return, courage moves us past it. The word "courage" derives from the Latin cor, which means heart. It's no coincidence that the quality of being that allows us to approach our fears, to build healthy emotional boundaries, and to live a purpose-driven life is one of heart.

Courage, of course, is risk and situation dependent. You might need it to leave a relationship or start your own business—but not to tie your shoelaces. That's to say, cultivating courage helps us do what's hard especially when we don't want to do it.

Remember, there's inherent risk to all those who go their own way. The good news is that courage is the skill that you get to practice every day for the rest of your life. Apply it over and over until it becomes so automatic, so hardwired, it is no different than riding a bicycle.

The poet and philosopher Goethe once said: "To put your ideas into action is the most difficult thing in the world." Courage is the power to do it anyway.

CHAPTER 4

MANAGE FEAR—CULTIVATING COURAGE

"Fearlessness is empowered by fear. You can't develop fearlessness—real compassionate fearlessness—without fear. Fearlessness is born of fear."

— JOHN DAIDO LOORI

I once had a young client by the name of Roger. He was a college dropout turned hotshot entrepreneur who experienced prodigious success in his online business. Global brands hired him regularly and coveted his time and advice.

Being something of a man in demand, Roger got invited to many evening galas and club parties. Pretty women attended these parties. This presented Roger with a problem: he was short and usually the youngest one there. He believed both to mean he was somehow undesirable.

His solution? Find a good corner, plop down with the other wallflowers, and sulk. Probably drink too much and talk nasty to himself, as well. And no, it wasn't even the *good, fun*–nasty kind of way, in case that's what you're thinking.

What's more, when Roger's collaborators felt obliged to introduce him to other people, Roger would act weirdly or say things that embarrassed all those present. Finally, after enough social shaming, he got fed up and called me for support.

Roger explained, "I feel like a failure every time I go to events like this; I want to talk to people, but I get scared. Then my heart beats so fast, and my palms get sweaty, and I worry so much that I won't know what to say, or I'll say too much, or the wrong thing… so I just stopped saying anything at all. It doesn't matter though. The pretty women don't like me. I'm too small for them. And I'm not *alpha* enough to hang with the other guys."

I had heard similar fear-talk and limiting beliefs from other clients but still needed to gather more information. " Hmm. Tell me more, Roger."

"It's happened a few times before. I've been introduced to a woman, we're talking, and then a guy who is bigger and stronger or cooler just comes over and interrupts the conversation. She turns her attention to him, and I end up just standing there like a third wheel. I wait around for a while, being ignored, and then I just back out and leave. It's embarrassing. Meeting new people sucks."

As we got into the specifics of his story, it became clear there were a few separate themes to work on, which we did, over time. Roger needed new conversational skills and to learn how to work a room and stay present in his body and aware of his surroundings while doing so.

But equally important—and perhaps at the core of his story—was that Roger just got too damn scared when he was out of his comfort zone and didn't know what to do about it. Can you perhaps relate? I know an earlier version of me certainty would.

THE EVOLUTIONARY EQUALIZER

One of the most common human experiences is fear. We all carry some fear of change, criticism, being alone, or—the mother of all fears—death.[21] [22] But even if we are all scared creatures, not everyone fears the same things or experiences fear in the same way.[23]

Suppose, for example, you had a fear of dentists: you'd be considered a *dentophobic*. (This fear isn't as unusual as you might think.)

---

21 Around 400 people around the world have Urbach-Wiethe disease. They literally, feel no fear—and biologically can't. Calcium deposits around the amygdala in the brain—the area critical for processing fear—interrupts this natural emotion for them, while permitting them to feel everything else—anger, joy, sadness—just not fear.

22 Karl Albrecht, "The (Only) 5 Fears We All Share."

23 "Can I Be Afraid of Phobias? Common or Unique Fears Explained."

Or suppose you feared clowns, you'd be *coulrophobic.*

Or suppose, instead, you feared ugliness: you'd be *cacophobic.*

And what about if you feared flowers—yes, those people exist, too—you'd be *anthophobic.*

Now, suppose you spotted an ugly, flower-holding dentist, dressed as a clown.

Well, then you'd probably just be fu*ked.

Or would you?

FEAR: FOE OR SECRET FRIEND?

Our societal ethos around fear is extreme. For example, we gate our communities. We install alarms. We take out large insurance policies. We teach our kids not to talk to strangers. We believe by making fear the enemy, we can spend our lives avoiding it. As a result, we rarely manage to deal with our fear as individuals. Do any of the following ring true for you?

- You use alcohol, sex, drugs, TV, or social media to numb yourself.
- You create the worst-case scenario in your head and use it as an excuse to not act.
- You're constantly stressed about something.
- You reply yes when you mean no, or no when you mean yes.
- You avoid meeting new people or trying new things.

- You daydream about a different, more adventurous or exciting life.
- You settle.

AN IMPORTANT DISTINCTION

Interestingly, former President Roosevelt once said, "The only thing we have to fear is fear itself." However, he appears to have been misinformed: fear itself is actually not the problem.

Fear is just negative arousal—an evolutionary program deep inside your reptilian brain that gets you to pay attention and act. It comes factory-installed for a reason; it's the power that keeps you alive in the face of the unknown.

However, to Roosevelt's point, if left unmanaged, fear can make us do weird things—as in flee and seek protection (flight) and draw our weapons (fight).

This is where it gets tricky. The risk for those of us who automatically seek protection when scared is that we live so cautiously, we might as well not have lived at all. On the other hand, the risk for those of us who automatically reach for our weapons is that we will never find a weapon big enough to make us feel safe. To truly be able to go your own way, then, the only solution is to change your relationship with the underlying emotion. And this change obviously takes place on the inside.

MANAGING YOUR FEAR

To be clear, managing fear is not about becoming physically stronger or more aggressive or even stoic. Rather, it's about two things: learning how to change your mental monologue and shifting the way your emotions move in your body. What does that mean, exactly? Let me explain by continuing Roger's story.

During our coaching work, Roger made it clear that whenever he met someone new—as in, outside of his familiar business settings or friend group—his social anxiety would take over. At that point, he would climb into his head and start telling himself things like: *You'll never be good enough. It doesn't matter what you achieve. You'll never be big and strong or man enough. A pretty girl would never want to be with someone like you. You shouldn't be here. No one actually likes you, they just like you for your business skills. You're actually a loser, a nobody.*

Funnily enough, some of the things he repeated to himself every day embarrassed him to voice aloud. Isn't it strange how poorly we sometimes treat ourselves sometimes?

Once he became aware of how his mental monologue was part of the problem, I taught him some self-coaching skills to change the conversation in his head.

For starters, I showed him how to slow down enough to monitor his mental monologues in real-time and notice his triggers.

This might sound like him saying to himself: "*When X happened, I thought/responded with Y*" and looking for patterns in the results.

After that, I encouraged him to turn his monologue into a mental dialogue by asking himself clarifying questions. For example, his self-generated feedback might sound like: "*Is X true? What evidence do I have? If X is not true, what else could it be? What would be a more desirable outcome (Y)?*" The latter questions would also help him generate behavioral alternatives for the strategies that weren't working for him.

Finally, we worked on learning to move emotions in his body. Moving through fear and building inner strength through the "felt-experience" is often faster than using words alone. At that point, I taught Roger my Courage Spin Technique to help him better manage his social fear, but you can apply it for just about any fear you may have. Here's how:

THE REBEL COURAGE SPIN

The exercise started with me asking, "Think of the situation. Connect to the emotion; which emotion is it? And where does that emotion originate inside your body?" (Your forehead? Your toenails?)

Roger replied, "My belly. It's fear. I'm afraid."

"Where does it go next?" I asked. "Where does it end up?"

Roger pointed to his chest as the final destination. "It moves up here."

Since people rarely report emotions as static and more often as cyclical, I had him describe the motion he was experiencing in that area. I used my index finger to make tiny clockwise or counterclockwise circles to indicate the direction the "energy of fear" might be moving.

"Which way is the fear emotion spiraling?" I asked. "For example, is it moving left to right, up and down or somehow differently?"

Then I asked Roger to show me with his index finger.

He made a clockwise circular motion with his finger about six inches in front of his belly. We then gave fear a color, so as to involve his visual sense, too.

"Red," Roger said. "Fear is a spinning red ball inside my belly."

"Good, now imagine pulling all that red fear a few inches outside of your body and seeing it out there in front of you." I pointed to a place a few inches in front of him, indicating what it might look like to pull the fear out of his body in front of him. "Once it gets out in front of you, if it randomly forms a representation or a picture or a symbol of some sort—that's fine, too."

"Just a molten ball of red for right now," Roger said, squeamishly.

For some, this step takes a bit more imagination.

"Great. Remember, this is just an imaginary exercise. Feel as much or as little of this as is right for you to get the lesson but consciously decide how much. Feeling only ten percent is also ok."

His face calmed.

"Now, with that molten red ball of fear out in front of you, notice what direction it's spinning, and for a few seconds, spin it faster in that direction. Then tell me what you feel."

"I feel more afraid. The ball got bigger."

This, by the way, is normal; people often comment that spinning the energy in the old direction intensifies the fear or emotion.

"Well, then, how about we change directions and feel something different? When you're ready, reverse the direction and spin it fast the other way."

He closed his eyes again and followed along.

"Now as you're spinning, spin it so fast in that new direction that maybe you get a color change. Or maybe the ball shrinks, or even transforms into something different. If your deeper mind wants to present you with a gift at the end, in the form of a picture or symbol to remind you that your fear has been transformed, let it do so."

He seemed to be visualizing intensely. His head was making tiny bobbing movements and his eyelids fluttered. He was silent for about a minute or so.

Then his shoulders visibly started to rise and fall, indicating deeper breathing. Tears streamed down his face. People often find that once they quickly spin their old fears in a new direction, their fear transforms, and they can actually feel good.

It's a touching realization that they don't have to suffer like they used to and that all future suffering is optional.

"Very good. Now, if you haven't already, pull the gift or the changed shape back into your body and fill the space where the old emotion used to be. And remember to breathe while you do so."

He lowered his head, eyes still closed. And sat quietly for a few minutes. When he opened them, he spoke slowly. "When I started to spin the red ball of fear in the other direction really fast, it started to turn blue and then shrink. When you told me to keep spinning it, I did until it randomly became a picture of a king chess piece. Then I pulled that image into my belly."

"Amazing. What does that representation of the king chess piece mean to you?"

"Strength and power. Like I can be myself when I'm at these events and meeting people, the same way I am when I'm consulting with my clients."

"That's right. So now if you were to imagine going to your next social event and having that king chess piece with you and then engaging people in that way, the way that is right for you, what do you feel?

"Powerful. Like a king. As if the whole place is mine."

"Great. Check back also into your chest. Is there anything left to clean up there or anywhere else in your body?"

"No, chest feels good, calm. So does my body. Thank you."

The bottom line is this: as long as things are changing in our environment, fear will always be nearby. However, by managing your mental monologue and applying the Rebel Courage Spin, you can now not only change how you feel in a matter of minutes or less but also the relationship you have with this vital, life-saving emotion in the first place. If you want to get started right now, make a list of what causes fear inside you—and then get spinning.

"God will not have his work made manifest by cowards."

— RALPH WALDO EMERSON

THE REBEL'S COURAGE SPIN PROCESS WILL MAKE YOU STRONGER (RECAP)

1. Think of your fear or disempowering emotion. Name it. Say it out loud.
2. Notice the feelings in your body. What direction are they moving? Give them a color.
3. Pull them out in front of you. If you prefer to give your fear a symbol or picture, imagine that floating in front of you.

4. Decide what way the picture or symbol is spinning, clockwise or counterclockwise. (If fear is motionless, ask: in what direction would it spin, if it could?)
5. Test what it feels like to spin it faster in that direction. Then spin it the opposite direction, faster and faster, until the color changes and/or the image disappears.
6. Once the image disappears, ask your deeper mind to give you a *gift*—some resource or picture that will serve you better than that old fear ever could.
7. Imagine enjoying the gift in the future, while back in the old, triggering environment. If the reaction is not changed to positive or neutral, repeat steps one through six.

(This process was inspired by Hallbom's Dynamic Spin Release technique.)

REBEL CASE STUDY:

The great Russian writer, Fyodor Dostoyevsky, was born in 1821. You might say his life had two distinct parts: before and after his imprisonment and mock execution.[24]

In the first part of his life, he produced some early literary works that earned him some success, and he spent his free time socializing with Russia's intelligentsia and other sophisticates. He was a tad shy and vain.[25]

However, in 1847, growing increasingly resentful of the circles he frequented, he joined the Petrashevsky Circle, a secret revolutionist group that circulated illegal propaganda. Two years later, he and the other members of the group were arrested, imprisoned, and sentenced to death.

When Dostoyevsky was brought to Semyonovsky Square on December 22, 1849, he was led to believe that the prisoners were going to be executed by firing squad. At the last moment, however, the guards lowered their guns and the prisoners' lives were spared.[26]

For Dostoyevsky, facing his death was the deepest encounter with fear that he had at that point experienced—until he was sent to a Siberian prison camp, that is. There, evil criminals,

---

24 Robert Greene, *The 50th Law.* (127–128)

25 Ibid.

26 Gary Saul Morson, "Fyodor Dostoyevsky."

filth and indecency, and cruelty from the guards were a harrowing and daily experience.[27]

However, these experiences connected him with the Russian peasantry in a way he didn't expect. These were precisely the poor people from whom, earlier in life, he had kept himself isolated. In a weird way, the time Dostoyevsky spent in the prison camp humanized him.

Four years later, he left the camp. This departure marked the second part of his life. Gone from his eyes were the hints of sparkly romanticism. What remained was the hardened spirit of an awakened—and henceforth skeptical—man.

From then onward, Dostoyevsky "regenerated" his beliefs around how society worked. For starters, he viewed the condescension and materialism of Russia's intelligentsia as a feeble protection from fear. This fear kept them separate from the basic goodness of the common people—and he'd had enough.[28]

In a subtle act of creative rebellion, fueled perhaps by a mix of frustration and vengeance—Dostoyevsky funneled his latest life experiences into a new series of literary works. During this period, he produced the popular *Crime and Punishment* and *The Brothers Karamazov* among many others. Such efforts reflected his profound psychological understanding of the deepest and darkest struggles of the human condition. What's more, by adapting his own horrific stories into

---

27 Ibid.

28 Ibid.

compelling fictional tales that benefited the greater good, Dostoyevsky indirectly altered how we relate to our fear and understand our humanity. If that's not rebellious, I don't know what is. Today, Dostoyevsky's creations live on in a class of their own.

CHAPTER 5

SEEK MEANING, THEN MONEY—FINDING PURPOSEFUL WORK

"Work is love made visible. The goal is not to live forever; the goal is to create something that will."

— JOHN DAIDO LOORI

In 2004, the Olympic Games made a historic return to their country of birth: Greece. The motto of the Games that year was "Welcome Home." Ironically, this happened to be the only year I wasn't going "home" to see the Greek side of my family. My grandfather persuaded my parents not to bring my sister and me to Greece due to a possible "act of terrorism" in Athens at the time.

The only act of terrorism is the one happening in your head, Papou. Now, I miss the Games and don't get to see you or the family.

What did I do instead? I got myself a consolatory desk job in the States. Having never worked for a company before, I told myself, *This, at least, will be a chance to try something different.*

Prior to that, I had only worked for myself. I ran a small eBay business reselling things online that I found in physical stores and made a nice margin. The desk-job company that hired me liked my business model and wanted me to do the same thing with their overstock.

Shortly after I got started at the job, however, the eBay project stalled. Suddenly, I found myself sitting in a chair, doing nothing, and getting paid for it. The fidgety teenage entrepreneur in me found this unnatural and weird. Shouldn't I be taking some packages somewhere or selling something?

First days, then weeks went by like that. Each day would bleed into the numbness of the next. It was not soon thereafter that my morale dropped, followed by my overall engagement at work.

Strangely, this fact seemed to affect (and be registered by) exactly none of my colleagues. They would just periodically look over, smile and nod slowly, as if to say: "That's right, kid, stay exactly where you are and don't push the pace."

When I thought I might go mad, I started looking for new ways to "pass the time." Article reading seemed like a good one. Get paid to learn? Ok, so maybe there was something interesting I could do at this company, after all.

That was, until many weeks (and articles) later, when my manager finally came around with something urgent for me to do.

"Ok, got a task for ya. So you're gonna take these here little plastic bottles and fill them with the Windex from this big bottle right over here. You got that?"

I looked over at a table covered with hundreds of little empty bottles and my mental monologue started up:

This isn't what I signed up for. At all. This place is a dead end. Plus, I kind of enjoy this article reading thing, and I've got a backlog of articles waiting to be read by me. Can't you just ask one of my colleagues to fill your bottles?

The response that came out of my mouth, however? "Yes, sir."

And thus started the beginning of the end.

* * *

This is what the next five days at the company looked like:

Day 1:

I start reading sports articles online.
Two hours pass.
I've done none of my bottle work.
Result: I stay late until I've finished filling all my bottles.

Day 2:

I start reading sports articles online.
I tell myself I'll only spend a minute on this article.
Two hours pass.
Result: I stay late until I've finished filling all my bottles.

Day 3:

My cousin (an athlete) sends me an email with a sports article link.
I click the link.
On second thought, I quickly close the browser.
Result: I do my work and leave on time.

Day 4:

It's the historic Closing Ceremonies—so many articles to follow!
I unplug my computer.
Result: I do my work and leave on time.

Day 5:

I decide to stop reading articles at work. I take it as a sign that it's time to find a more engaging way to use my life instead.

WAYS WE WASTE TIME

There are only so many working hours between sunrise and sunset. Regardless of how you use them, do any of these ring true for you?

- You're disconnected to the bigger mission of what you're doing.
- You believe engagement is the job's responsibility, not yours.
- You believe managing time is your boss's responsibility, not yours.
- You start working on tasks without thinking about the how or why.

If you said yes to any of the above, the following paragraphs are going to show you how you can get more meaning out of your day and life.

WE ACTUALLY DON'T HAVE THAT MUCH TIME TO WASTE

Time is our most precious resource. It's also the great equalizer: we all have the same number of hours in a day—whether billionaire or babysitter.

Time has always fascinated me because of its influence over us. What else can make you feel guilty about the past, anxious about the future, and annoyed with the present all at once? (Ok, aside from your mother.) That is to say, time is directly related to your inner strength and freedom at the most basic of levels; if you don't take charge of it, it takes charge of you.

MAKING THE MOST OF YOUR TIME

When I was in middle school, I spent almost 1,000 hours volunteering at a local retirement home. I didn't plan to do that many hours—what sane kid would?—my parents got me the gig. I'm guessing they saw it as "free" and "morally-constructive."

I, on the other hand, experienced it as a weird blend between afterschool, adult-daycare, and a minimum-security prison—with a funny smell. And yet, even after the first few months, I kept going back.

Time spent there was mostly in the company of the elderly (surprise), wheeling them around and helping set up for their events. The unintended side effect of spending time with lots of slow-moving people—who have more life behind them than ahead of them—is you learn to slow down yourself. And listen. Patiently.

Another side effect was, during those three years, I probably had hundreds of conversations with the elderly about what matters in life. They loved to share, so I got to hear the joys and pains, the love and loss of it all. Still, I couldn't help but wonder if after being pent up in those facilities for so long, would they have welcomed anyone with a sympathetic ear, semi-active mind, and resting heart rate above twenty beats per minute?

Before I graduated middle school, I was asked to write a report citing what I had learned from my time spent serving the elderly. I wrote (paraphrased): *From Steven, I learned that for a relationship to work, you have to be prepared to sacrifice at least fifty percent of who you think yourself to be, and it's still worth it. Mr. Michaels, whose legs don't work anymore, told me to go travel and see the world while I still can. Candice, once a devout painter who is now blind, told me to dedicate myself to doing what I love, while I still can. And Albert reminded me every day that life is like a roll of toilet paper, the closer you get to the end, the faster it goes. Nearly all of them said they wished they had spent more time with their friends and family while they could. And that eating retirement-home food sucks.*

RE-EVALUATING HOW YOU SPEND MOST OF YOUR DAYS

We spend roughly one-third of our lives working and another one-third sleeping. Something is off if, in between the two, much of your life looks like this:

- You spend too many weeks or months in a row doing something you don't enjoy.
- You don't believe in the cause of the thing that you're doing.
- You regularly spend much of your day in a negative thought cycle thinking about how things could have been or should be different.
- Stress and exhaustion have become normal states of being for you.
- You're not having fun or learning, and work feels like emotional labor for you.
- You feel like you're wasting your time and the "treadmill" is leading nowhere.

Admittedly, people living on the fringe of poverty supporting their families by working minimum wage jobs amidst an economic downturn, for example, may see little opportunity to change the above. But for most of the rest of us, there is nothing utopian about finding and enjoying meaningful work. You must do *something* with the hours you're not sleeping or pissing around; you might as well make them meaningful.

PURPOSEFUL WORK WILL MAKE YOU STRONGER

REBEL TIPS FOR LIVING & WORKING MEANINGFULLY

ENJOY YOUR YOUTH BEFORE WORRYING ABOUT MEANING

Most people spend around five decades or so of their lives working. Translation: if you're in your twenties or early thirties, you've still got plenty of time to get focused. So, if circumstances permit, explore! Try fun jobs, pursue weird hobbies, approach and talk to strangers, travel internationally, learn a foreign language, experiment with drugs, alcohol, and casual sex if so inclined, ride motorcycles and skydive. You're bound to end up getting some clues about what would make work and life meaningful for you along the way.

DECIDE YOU CARE ENOUGH TO DO SOMETHING ABOUT IT

If you are already well into your career or feel stuck in some uninspiring job, the first step is to decide if it's worth the effort to change. Let's be realistic: it will take time and energy to do so. On the other hand, this dilemma won't go away by filling little Windex bottles until the end of time.

Move generally toward your inspiration

If you're unclear about what you want to do, you don't need to be overly specific when considering your next career step. To give you an analogy, if you live in Maine and want to end up in Florida, all you need to do to start is head south. Having a specific destination gets important only as you get closer. Finding meaningful work is no different. Start with a general idea of what you want from your work. Then dive deeper into the job descriptions to which you find yourself magnetized. Details can come later.

Find the intersection between values and talents

Imagine you never had to worry about money again. What would you do? A simple exercise for this is to draw a square on a piece of paper. In one of each of the corners, list your passions, talents, values, and dreams. Then think about possible professions that would connect the four of them. Write those in the center of the square.[29]

Choose a profession that fosters learning

Find a job that lets you read sports articles all day! Just kidding. But you might want to pursue work that encourages you to learn and grow. Developing your personal and professional skills while getting a paycheck buys you time and perhaps some more clarity. Not to mention, you'll create a broader, more diverse skillset.

---

29 Justin Faerman, "The Eight Keys to Finding Meaningful Work."

Keep the passion alive

If you intend to stay in your current line of work but need a change, ask: what could I do to bring back the passion? Maybe organize an event or join a socially responsible initiative of your choice. If you're really set on staying where you are, maybe there's a lateral move within the company that would reinvigorate you. If not, consider getting a little deeper with the people with whom you work. You may realize you actually know very little about them. Such connective conversations are free and can happen anytime.

Tomorrow is a new day

Whether you're working with a computer in an office or caring for the elderly in a retirement home, we all have the same twenty-four hours in a day. On average, you'll have about 28,500 of such days over the span of your life, if you're American or European.[30] What this means is if you're a thirty-something reading this book, you still have, on average, another 17,000 chances to try again. Didn't get it right today? Start organizing your life the way you want it tomorrow.

"The aim of life is to live, and to live means to be aware, joyously, drunkenly, serenely, divinely aware."

— HENRY MILLER

30 "Life Expectancy at Birth, Total (Years) - United States | Data."

REBEL CASE STUDY:

Benjamin Franklin was born into a family of candle makers in Boston in the early 1700s. By the time he was twelve, his father Josiah Franklin expected his son to start learning the family business so that he could one day take over. But Benjamin had other plans. He liked words. He wanted to learn his brother's printing business.

This surprised Josiah. He knew it would mean more and harder work for young Benjamin, plus a nine-year apprenticeship learning the printing business instead of one that lasted seven. But Benjamin didn't want to make candles for the rest of his days; he wanted to make headlines. His dream was to become a writer. If it meant learning to do so while handling printing machines with lots of manual labor—so be it.

The apprenticeship turned out to be good for Benjamin. In addition to his regular duties, he read books and copy-edited articles. He also started overseeing the reprinting of English newspaper articles and learned to imitate their style in his own writing. By the end of his apprenticeship, Benjamin knew how to run a printing business and was a competent writer himself.

But Benjamin wanted more action and grew antsy to apply his skills. When his brother, James, was about to launch a newspaper called *The New-England Courant*, Benjamin presented him with some interesting story ideas. James could have cared less and ignored his brother's musings.

That's when Benjamin shifted strategies. Applying a little cunning, he crafted the stories under the pseudonym of Silence Dogood—a fictional, strong-minded widow. He then sent them to *The Courant*, where they were published and became an instant sensation.[31]

But the dishonest success weighed heavily on his conscience. After some time, Benjamin confessed that he was actually the brains behind Mrs. Dogood's letters, and James was furious. Their relationship subsequently soured.[32]

From there, Benjamin decided to leave Boston, ditching his position at the newspaper and turning his back on his family altogether. He settled in Philadelphia, where he got a short-lived job at a printing shop in town. Soon, he was on his way to England. Unfortunately, only after making the transatlantic journey and arriving in London did he realize that the business proposition that brought him there was illegitimate.

Stuck in a foreign country with no prospects, Benjamin was at a bit of a crossroads. He could make the long voyage home and try and start over, or he could use the opportunity to explore the UK. Both options had their benefits and costs. Ultimately, Benjamin chose to see what he could learn working at a large-scale printing shop in England. Two years later—after he had gotten his fill of company, country, and

31 Robert Greene, *Mastery.* (148-152)

32 Ibid.

culture— he returned to Philadelphia. That's when his career took off.

It seems his wanderings served him well; upon returning, in a spurt of unprecedented creativity, Benjamin launched his own printing and publishing business. He then pivoted into the field of science and made many great inventions. His career would ultimately evolve again, bringing him into the field of politics. Of course, along the way, he achieved his dream of becoming a best-selling writer as well.

Looking back, you might call Benjamin the consummate rebel: he resisted pre-existing structures and was constantly meddling to find his own. In his case, you might say it wasn't about defining, but rather about *redefining*, his own way every so often. But this is just what it took for Benjamin to develop meaning for himself during a long and ultimately distinguished career.

CHAPTER 6

STAND UP TALL—EMBODYING STRENGTH

"When I was trying to be the best poker player in the world, basically, I would play anyone, at any stage... and that's just something that I didn't really find a lot of happiness in. It takes sacrifice to get to the top of the poker world and stay there... I put way too much stress and pressure on myself to perform and keep putting up results. It's something that I've had trouble with over my career, and it's given me constant anxiety—plus all the hours I spent in a simulated environment... I feel like it just kind of messed me up.

So that's what got me into taking care of my mind and body much more seriously than ever with yoga, meditation, nutrition, sleep, all of it—just trying to be happy. Poker takes a toll on your brain and your body... to play five, six days a week for thirteen years in a row; I take that side of the game [i.e. wellness] more seriously now."

—GREG MERSON, 2012 WORLD SERIES OF POKER (WSOP) MAIN EVENT WINNER (WINNINGS WELL OVER $8.5 MILLION)

We can all relate to at least some part of Greg's story above. Excelling at anything requires dedication and sacrifice. But his story also reminds us that the body is more than a mere instrument for achievement. His story reminds us that sacrificing the body—while common in our society—is the wrong sacrifice. Why do we so often end up abusing these magnificent machines?

For starters, it's culturally approved to ignore the body; we celebrate intellect and emotions as more important, instead. Moreover, our lives are sedentary, with movement being the exception but not the rule. Meanwhile, busyness and stress also leave us limp and contracted, with our attention frayed.

On the other hand, we might focus on building bulging biceps and washboard abs, because they'll get us more Instagram likes. However, while scrolling on social media, we often over-identify with "perfect" images of the human form and learn to comparatively hate our own. Thus, the cycle continues.[33]

This happens because we're disconnected with what goes on inside the body: a majestic symphony of 650 or so muscles

33 Mark Walsh, *Embodiment: Moving Beyond Mindfulness.* (41)

that sit atop a stack of 206 bones, under which 11 bodily systems pump your blood, digest your food, and breathe your air—without asking for much at all. We've also overlooked that the body is the doorway to the sensations of life: feelings, shapes, postures, rhythms, and dynamics. Moreover, we've forgotten that the body is the home where safety, power, and inner strength begin or—in the case of bad health and emotional issues—stop.[34]

Finally, we've missed that the body is closer to something you are, as opposed to something you have.

WE TREAT OUR BODIES LIKE SECOND-RATE CITIZENS

Churchill once said that we shape our buildings; thereafter we shape us. I think the same is true for our bodies. We shape them with our habits and thoughts and behaviors and, in turn, they influence the quality of our lives.

Do any of the following ring true for you?

- You spend a lot of time bowing your neck down or looking up to a screen of some sort.
- Movement is something narrowly reserved for the gym and best done in sets of three.
- If you run on a treadmill, you do so while reading a magazine or watching TV.
- You pop a pill at the slightest backache or pain but do nothing to realign or stretch your body.

---

34 Ibid.

- You subscribe to the "work hard, play hard" philosophy but always forget the "rest hard" bit.
- You've outsourced concern for your body to some doctor or "authority," as if they know your body better than you do.
- You treat your body like a dutiful Uber for your brain.

WE'VE BEEN LOOKING AT STRENGTH AND THE BODY ALL WRONG

When it comes to strength and the body, the question is not if you go to the gym for an hour a day or not. The real question is what do you do with (and in) your body for the other twenty-three hours of the day?

Think about the larger relationship you have with your body:

- Do you sit for eight hours or more per day, probably in a chair, like twenty-five percent of Americans do? [35]
- When you sit, what happens to your posture? Do your shoulders round; does your pelvis tilt and spine sag?
- Do you clench your diaphragm and restrict your breath?
- How about your pelvic floor muscles and anus—are they also constantly clenched and protectively holding onto stress?
- Have you ever even *tried* to let your "armpits drop" and belly plop as a way of relaxing?

---

35 Alice Park, "Most Americans Spend Way Too Much Time Sitting Down. Here's How to Avoid Being One of Them."

- When you feel tired, depleted, or maybe even lonely—do you substitute eating, drinking, smoking, shopping, sex, or social media for self-care?
- Do you find your awareness existing only in the space behind your eyes but disconnected from, say your feet? Are you even feeling your feet right now?

REAL STRENGTH IS ABOUT MUCH MORE THAN THAT

Real strength is about building a life around your body—not the other way around. It's about prioritizing movement and mobility, much as our agrarian ancestors did. It's about holding your body in a way that is upright and elegant, not contracted or hunched. On another level, as embodiment expert Mark Walsh says, it's about recognizing the body as the most accessible part of our being, worthy of empowerment and inner strength. This is our operating system. This is our autobiography. This is the body.

WHY YOU INSTINCTIVELY KNOW HOW TO DO THIS ALREADY

The interplay between movement and emotion is profound. Here's a story to explain what I mean.

Years ago, I found myself in a long hall in India teaching an embodiment workshop to a room full of yogis. Because of my coaching background and as a long-time yogi myself, we explored how this ancient methodology could be leveraged for personal empowerment (i.e. building inner strength).

During the demonstration, I had all the participants, minus two, stand at the top of their mats and adopt a neutral, relaxed standing stance, whatever that meant to them. (I think I called it "*Tadasana* on vacation.")

Meaning, the other two yogis—the *control variables* in my workshop example—were instructed to walk up and down the corridor and just *look* at people without talking.

"Scan their faces and bodies. Get a baseline reading of your classmates."

Once they felt they got a "sense" of the workshop participants, I asked them to step outside the Yoga Shala and wait.

In the meantime, I had everyone in the room think of a time in their lives that they felt disempowered or weak. "A maximum of a five on a ten scale in terms of intensity," I said. Then I asked them to: a) feel the experience in their bodies and b) let their bodies ease into some representative asana or body "sculpture."

The vibe of the room shifted completely; some people got into warrior positions. Others stood on one leg and wobbled. Others, still, lowered themselves into a squatting *Malasana* position and put their hands protectively over their heads or faces. A few people assumed the fetal position.

At that point, I called the *control* participants back in.

"Look around. In a few words, what do you notice?"

After a long pause, one of them said, "Everyone seems smaller and more bunched up."

The other control then added, "Also a little off-balance... and frustrated."

I thanked them and sent them back outside. The "controls" had no idea what I'd told the group.

Then I turned back to the group. "Now think of a time you felt totally strong and empowered. When you've got it, let your body ease into your "strong" sculpture."

The room again morphed. Many of the people who were sitting, stood. Those who were crouching reached for the sky. The wobblers put the other foot down and created a wider base. Many people smiled, and almost everyone spread their arms and legs in some fashion, becoming more expansive.

When I brought the *controls* back in for their final round of observational feedback, they looked at the group again and this time said: "Bigger," "stronger," and "more peaceful and beautiful."

The point of this exercise was to have participants explore the two-way street between their bodies and being. What they don't often realize before this exercise is that observing how they move is a way of observing how they feel, and similarly, that changing the way they move directly changes how they feel.[36] So when someone decides to "stand up tall" or "take

---

36 Mark Walsh, *Embodiment: Moving Beyond Mindfulness.* (42)

up space"—literal examples of inner strength, embodied—it changes the way they feel about themselves, too.

Applied for our purposes here, a rebel who is disconnected from their body will come to know true strength with great difficulty. So, spend some time with your body. Notice it. Feel its shapes. Slow down enough to savor the limits and possibilities contained within. Remember, your body is like an inner strength meter: it's constantly giving you data in the form of sensory feedback, letting you know when you are off course and guiding you back to your most natural, powerful, loving self.

STANDING UP TALL WILL MAKE YOU STRONGER

REBEL TIPS FOR EMBODYING STRENGTH

FIX YOUR SEAT

Most of us sit for much of the day. There's a right way to sit, and it's easy. The right way is with your weight evenly distributed across your sitz bones. To do this, standing with your rear facing the chair, put the index finger of each hand in the crease where your leg meets your hip—at your hip socket—and push your tailbone down and back until you slowly meet the seat. Rest your feet on the ground, establishing a natural base. As you do, point your tailbone down. This will ever so slightly rotate your pelvis and help you sit up straight in a relaxed, dignified, and strong way.[37]

---

37 Paul Linden, *Breakfast Essays: Brief Writings on Body Awareness and Life*. (61–63)

Aim for body symmetry

Mark Walsh points out that fashion models are often photographed with slanted shoulders, jutting chins, tilted heads, and twerked necks. This is considered "cool." In this case, cool is not necessarily a strong body; body symmetry, on the other hand, is strong. Unaligned body posture, held for years, is just a future visit to the chiropractor. Remember, a long spine is a strong spine.

Start a practice that engages your body and mind

Drop that magazine, put down your cell phone, and find an "embodied" practice. Yoga, dance, and martial arts are all things that will get you routinely moving, breathing, and sensing all at once. The idea here is not just to move, but to regularly expand your awareness beyond the space behind your eyes and into the rest of that flesh-puppy.

Then build your day around that practice (instead of the other way around)

Years ago, I had to put "TIME WITH BODY" on my calendar once a day until my movement practice became habitual. Now starting and ending my day with a few minutes (or more when I have it) of movement and meditation helps me feel more connected to my body and show up stronger at work and home. Schedule yours in (with capital letters) if you have to.

Find your center as often as is necessary

A centered state of being is one in which you are grounded, connected, and compassionate.[38] Centering yourself helps calm the busy world and opens you up to new possibilities and states of strength. You can use the following technique to practice centering yourself in twelve seconds or less.

- Three seconds – Close your eyes. Inhale through your nose. At the top of your breath, hold.
- Three seconds – Tense every muscle in your body while holding your breath.
- Three seconds – Exhale and let go completely.
- Three seconds – Notice the tingle of gravity bringing you back to earth.

Play (and circulate) your attention

During the interims and short delays that you inevitably experience throughout the day, try moving your attention around the inside of your body. For example, while waiting in line to check out at the supermarket, I might deliberately put all my attention on my right foot. And just keep it there. Then I explore: how does the bottom of my foot (plantar) feel pushing into the ground? What about the top of my foot (*dorsum*), pressing against the top of my shoe? What about the other foot? Then, how evenly is my weight distributed between my feet? 50/50? 40/60? 10/90(!)?

---

38 Wendy Palmer and Janet Crawford, *Leadership Embodiment: How the Way We Sit and Stand Can Change the Way We Think and Speak*, (12–14)

Also, can I keep my awareness in my feet while deliberately spreading it to my knees? What about my hips, belly, and torso? This exercise helps me return to my body when I've spent a long time paying attention to what's outside of it, in my environment.

Observe your feelings

Spend a few days noticing emotions in your body. Each time you experience a strong emotion, ask your body *where* it is and *what* is it doing. Do the same the next time you're connected to your inner strength. What's the associated bodily experience like? Learn to recognize its indelible signature within, so you can recall it more frequently.

"Your body isn't a temple, it's a home you'll live in forever. Take care of it."

— COLIN WRIGHT

REBEL CASE STUDY:

Theodore Roosevelt, the twenty-sixth President of the United States, was born in 1858 with a body that failed him. He would spend his entire life struggling with his terrible asthma, which often left him bedridden, breathless, and weak.

But in 1870, the "sorry little specimen,"[39] as Theodore was called, got particularly desperate—the massages and various electrical therapies he was getting just weren't working. So, one day his father sat him down and said, "Theodore, you have the mind, but you have not the body, and without the help of the body, the mind cannot go as far as it should. You must make your body. It is hard drudgery to make one's body, but I know you will do it."[40]

In that moment, something changed for young Theodore. It seems that as he was made aware of the connection between body and mind, his ideas for what his body could do also changed. To get started, he would need to discipline his mind. So, he began what he later called "the strenuous life"—a physically intense and active way of being. This approach would help him heal himself throughout his life.

That's not to say that his asthma ever went away. But for years, he used movement as a way to come into his body, even while he suffered from regular asthma attacks. What's more—for

39 David McCullough, *Mornings on Horseback*. (90)

40 Ibid. (112)

a long time—the bag-punching, dumbbell-lifting, and gymnastic activity he busied himself with did little good. The good thing about the exertion, however, was that it got him out of his head and into his body in a new way. Only then could his body truly bring him into the world.

The decades that followed were busy. He would eventually graduate Harvard, get married, lead a unit in the Spanish-American War, and serve as governor of New York.

However, things changed for Theodore on Valentine's day, 1884. While out attending to legislative business, he received an emergency call to come home to Long Island. It appeared that both his wife, Alice, and his mother, Martha—who lived with them—were dying.

Alice had developed a renal ailment called Bright's disease. Martha had come down with a severe case of typhoid fever. Within twenty-four hours of his returning to their bedsides—one on each floor of the house—they were both dead.

Theodore was understandably crushed. For a long time, the deaths of the most important women in his life haunted him. He could barely eat, think, or sleep. Finally, it became clear: if he were to survive this tragedy, he had to escape New York—and get into nature. He had to be with himself. He had to get in touch with his body, move it *strenuously*—and, hopefully, remember what it was like to feel alive.

After selling virtually everything he owned, he moved to a ranch in the Dakota Territories, perched right on the Missouri River. It was there, in the subzero, snowy winters and the mild summers, he spent most of his days working outside. It was there, on the open prairies, that he was able to move and breathe. It was there, amid the tall pines and mountain passes, that he started to grieve.

Theodore spent three years living like this—in a physically intense relationship with his body and nature. Ultimately, this is what it took for him to get into the heavy emotions that were tangled in his body, to cultivate the inner strength to return to the East and ultimately become President of the United States.

CHAPTER 7

DEFEND YOUR LIMITS—BUILDING PERSONAL BOUNDARIES

"A 'no' uttered from deepest conviction is better than a 'yes' merely uttered to please, or worse, to avoid trouble."

— MAHATMA GANDHI

My personal boundary work officially began in my early twenties. I was at a personal development conference in Brazil doing some filming work for the event producer. For some reason, seeing me working with my cameras, multiple attendees approached me asking if I could "*just film a little 'side video' for them... for free.*" They must have sensed my penchant for people-pleasing hanging in the air.

Despite my *numerous* hesitations, I said yes on multiple occasions. After all, I wanted to be the *likable* foreigner and make new friends. After the first couple requests, though, each yes became progressively more painful and multiplied my workload.

But what was I to do? I didn't want to hurt anyone's feelings. I didn't want to "reject" them. So instead, in true *resentful-victim form*, I told myself, "you'll find a way"—and I did, until the seventh request.

At that point, when my lips parted and I exhaled some garbled agreement to do more work, my teeth gritted, my body tightened, and droplets of sweat collected on my brow. The physical sensations were accompanied by a wave of resentment. First, for the person who made the request. Next, for myself. Finally, for the culture.

Why do people keep asking for stuff? Where are their manners!

To be clear, the real issue obviously wasn't cultural; it was personal. The difficulty with boundaries was my own.

Later that day, I met a coach at the event. Using the same mind-body techniques I would later come to learn myself, he helped me swap some of the underlying beliefs that made saying no so hard. This coach helped me see that I didn't owe anyone anything. That was just old rhetoric stemming from growing up with a family of people-pleasers. After my session, I approached the person who had last asked me for a handout and began setting myself free:

"I don't know how to say this, but here it goes. I over-spoke before. I'm too busy. I can't shoot a video for you. I'm sorry if this upsets you. But if I do this, it won't be good for either of us. I understand if you're mad, but I can't do this. Again, I'm sorry."

At that point, I was prepared for them to be furious. I had visions of them jamming two fingers into my eye sockets and in one clean pluck, pulling my eyes out.

Instead, what happened? Nothing. They barely blinked.

"*Ta bom, Eugenio, sem problema.*" (It's ok, Eugene, no problem).

And off they went.

There I stood, dumbfounded. No drama. No hard feelings. Just less unpaid work to do.

I felt like I had turned a corner in life.

BOUNDARIES

As Dr. Henry Cloud and Dr. John Townsend point out, boundaries inform every part of your life. They separate what is you from what is not you. Your skin, for example, is a basic physical boundary: it keeps your organs in and the pathogens out. Or, as described above, the word "no" is an example of an emotional and spiritual boundary. Using it regularly reminds people that you are autonomous and exist independently from *their* wants and agenda. Boundaries, whether physical, emotional, or spiritual help reinforce *your* needs, likes, desires—and help you be your own person.[41]

Healthy boundaries are requisite for going your own way. What does healthy, in this context, mean? It's different for everyone. Likely for you, "healthy" means you are not so hard and walled up that you can't express yourself or ask for help. But then again, nor are you so open that your brain is at risk of falling out.

I like to remember that even the world's most fortified castles have a draw bridge that can go up or down depending on who's on the other side.

HOW THIS HAPPENS

Boundaries aren't inborn. We develop them early in life. As I mentioned in Chapter 1, we all start out as helpless infants, totally dependent on our caretakers for food, changing, and safety. We learn our limits based on these significant early relationships. Eventually, as we grow, we may separate from these relationships but without our personal boundaries intact. Do any of these ring true for you?

- You feel guilty when saying "no."
- You've avoided setting a boundary, so you don't "hurt" or "upset" someone.
- You think only selfish people set boundaries.
- You avoid setting limits in order to avoid someone's strong reaction, i.e. anger.

---

41 Dr. Henry Cloud and Dr. John Townsend, *Boundaries.*

- You've repressed your own reaction to avoid getting into an argument.
- You've carried an emotional burden for a loved one.

WHY WE DON'T ENFORCE OUR BOUNDARIES

Fear is at the crux of most boundary issues, and it comes in many flavors:[42]

- You're afraid to be alone and having to be with yourself (so you stay in the wrong relationships).
- You're afraid to show your whole self: what if people don't like the real you?
- You're disconnected from your human value, so you seek approval instead.
- You're afraid of breaking rules or not seeming nice.
- You're afraid of feeling bad for not doing what people want.
- You're afraid of emotional retribution or the withdrawal of love.

The only way to manage this fear indefinitely is to seal your boundary gaps. If, on the other hand, you choose to let these gaps go unheeded, you run the risk of a lifetime of misery. People will treat you in a doormat-esque fashion. You'll do more work and expend more effort while doing it than is necessary. Your relationships won't be as genuine. You'll constantly feel like a shell or caricature of yourself, but you'll be so busy shuffling around, acting on behalf of others, that you won't have time to notice.

---

42 Ibid.

For example, I knew of a guy who studied for a decade to become a doctor. He took out hundreds of thousands of dollars in loans to do so. After years of studying to do something he knew he didn't like, he finally got his medical degree. That same evening, he went to the store and had it framed. Then, the next day, he presented it to his mother with a note:

Dear Mom, Here, it took me ten years, but I did this for you. Now I'm going to do something that I enjoy, for me.

And with that, his medical career was over and a new parental boundary was in place.

* * *

Your boundaries signal to others that you will not be pushed further or used for their agendas. When people sense your boundaries—whether through your demeanor, behavior, or words—they will understand that you have a "line" and it cannot be crossed. Conversely, if people can't sense that there are consequences for mistreating you, they will push you and take what they can. Such is human nature. And since you can't fault human nature, your best bet is to tighten up those boundaries.

Below you'll find some tips on how.

DEFENDING YOUR LIMITS WILL MAKE YOU STRONGER

REBEL TIPS FOR PERSONAL BOUNDARIES

CLARIFY YOUR VALUES

Decide what's important to you. Make a list. Then subordinate anything that's not in your top five values. Unfortunately, while living and studying with my mentors around the world, I spent years accepting guilt from others for my unconventional lifestyle choices. All that changed once I realized that my top values were growth, adventure, language-learning, and travel—and not social conformity, 8 a.m.–6 p.m. work schedules, and ten optional vacation days a year. I had been living aligned with my values all along, but because of a boundary gap, I spent years making myself feel bad for it.

SEIZE YOUR AUTONOMY

Even if you've spent a lifetime being mistreated by others, the simple truth is, at some point, you must take back your autonomy. No one is going to give it to you. And what would they be giving you, anyway? A certificate? A high-five? Membership to their Meet-Up group?

Autonomy happens inside your mind and body. Reclaim what is yours by birthright; seize it back. Just a note on that: if you have been abused or have physical trauma around this topic (statistics vary but often show at least one in every five typically do), these guidelines will help, but it's best to seek a trauma specialist for support through the integration process. You have every right in the world to enjoy your life, and if it didn't happen in childhood, you can begin the process today by getting the proper support.

STOP EXPLAINING

Stop justifying yourself. By decree of the invisible authority you already have—but maybe didn't realize—explanations of all types are henceforth optional.

This may sound strange, but you don't owe anyone anything—even family. Furthermore, if you feel a boundary-pusher homing in on you, skip their questions. Give yourself permission in advance to ignore their spiel, change the topic, and move on.

RECOGNIZE IT FASTER

Listen to people's choice of words. What do they seem to be saying, really? Learn to recognize guilt or shame messaging. As you build stronger boundaries, you'll be able to quickly identify when you're being controlled or manipulated. In most cases, manipulation happens through seemingly innocent language. (Remember the section on Weasel phrases in Chapter 1? It's very similar.) Ask yourself: how have I allowed myself to be manipulated in the past?

SLOW DOWN

One sign your boundaries have been pushed is a flare of sudden resentment or uneasiness in your body. If you feel either of these during a conversation with someone, slow down. Step away. Ask them to "hold the thought" and circle back.

Meanwhile, check-in with yourself. Think about the context: What will a yes or no cost you? What will I gain or lose from staying quiet on this? Feel into your body for confirmation. If you are more visual, close your eyes and imagine yourself saying yes: do you feel better, worse, or neutral?

BECOME A DEFAULT "NO"

Some people say yes too fast without considering what their *yes* actually entails. If that's you, save yourself the awkward cleanup in advance. Until you've moved through the inner work required of strengthening your personal boundaries or examined the case individually and decided it's something you fully want to do, let "no" be your default answer.

On a personal note, I've grown tremendously since my days giving away my time and energy for free. What's more, I now can spot a boundary-pusher almost instantly. The sentence that got me over the learning curve was: "Hey, sorry, that's not going to work for me, but if something changes on my side, I'll let you know."

PREPARE YOURSELF TO WALK AWAY

Manipulators can easily smell someone who is reestablishing their boundaries. They feel you reclaiming authority over your life—and they don't like it. Anticipate pushback from these people. Be clear on your breaking point. Meaning, what is the threshold, at which, if crossed, you'll walk away from the relationship, deal, event, etc.? If the thought of walking away stirs fear or a sense of loss in you, remember, there's always something better around the corner.

Assert yourself

Boundaries imply occasional confrontation. When done elegantly with a win-win attitude, confrontation builds relationships. While aggression is not necessary, mental preparation is recommended.

Be loving as you implement

As you start sealing boundary gaps, be kind to those who have overstepped your lines in the past. And pace yourself. Wanting to pick up the phone and call everyone who has wronged you since birth is, of course, understandable—but no need to blow up your life. Instead, take one relationship and/or conversation at a time. Maybe start with friends, in a safe context, before later moving to family, loved ones, and colleagues.

"Lack of boundaries invites lack of respect."

— ANONYMOUS

REBEL CASE STUDY:

Born in 1869, Mahatma Gandhi led India's independence movement against British rule. He was the chief engineer of the non-violent civil disobedience that would ultimately bring down the Crown.

The state of subjugation of the Indian people had long bothered Gandhi. He was astonished at their submissiveness and passivity to British rule as a country and collective.

In his *Autobiography*, he wrote "I came across tales of [the] Government's tyranny… what surprised me then, and what still continues to fill me with surprise, was the fact that a province… should have taken all these brutal excesses lying down."

Why had the Indian people allowed such atrocities? Was his a nation of people without individual and collective boundaries? Many explanations existed: that Indians were weak, demoralized, unorganized, or had no weapons.

But Gandhi would only concern himself in discovering the answer after a personal incident in South Africa. Despite having a first-class ticket while traveling aboard a train, a white passenger demanded he leave the premium cabin. Gandhi refused and was forcibly thrown off the train at a station in Pietermaritzburg.

The experience offended him deeply. In fact, it offended his boundary to the degree that this otherwise quiet, unassuming man dedicated the rest of his life to "fighting the deep disease of color prejudice." This was the issue he found at the core of the British problem in his homeland as well.

Upon returning to India, he wrote, *My ambition is no less than to convert the British people through non-violence and thus make them see the wrong they have done to India.* [43]

He thus called for government officials to quit their jobs, students to quit going to government schools, soldiers to ditch their posts, and the public to stop paying taxes—and organized other mass boycotts.[44] Gandhi was imprisoned several times for spreading civil disobedience and ultimately murdered by extremists late in life.

However, in 1947—largely thanks to the efforts started by this man—India got her boundaries when she declared independence from the British Raj, once and for all.

43 Evan Andrews, "When Gandhi's Salt March Rattled British Colonial Rule."

44 "Mahatma Gandhi."

PART III

CONFIDENCE

"I am owner of my might, and I am so when I know myself as unique."

— MAX STIRNER

If you've gotten this far, you've already made the choice to go your own way. You've cultivated the courage to do what scares you, befriending your fear in the process.

Now, when confronting a challenge, you tell yourself "I can handle this," or "Let's see how I'm going to figure this out." If the task is particularly hard or complex, you think of all the past times you've gotten through tough things—and then you do it again. Confidence is nearby.

What is confidence, exactly? It is a generalized belief in your abilities. It's a trust in your decisions. It's a reliance on yourself with often a positive bias toward action.

Ultimately, confident people seem to have an air about them. A wave of positive, assertive calm. How you might develop a similar "*vibe*" varies, but I've found three of the biggest leverage points to be: your relationship with time, your relationship with control, and your relationship with yourself.

Let's now explore these topics in the next chapters.

CHAPTER 8

BECOME YOUR OWN PERSON—SELF-ACCEPTANCE

"We are free when our acts proceed from our entire personality, when they express it, when they exhibit that indefinable resemblance to it which we find occasionally between the artist and his work."

— HENRI BERGS

Erica was my first crush. She was tall, had cropped blond hair, and moved with the grace of a wild antelope. She was also smart. So smart, in fact, that on Valentine's Day in first grade, she took the heart-shaped box of chocolates that I had secretly placed in her cubby, read my handwritten card, and without skipping a beat, closed the card and placed the duo back in my cubby.

A plainer form of rejection, I do not know. I also can't remember if I watched this happen while sitting at my classroom desk or looking down from the ceiling, where my disembodied soul must have been floating. It didn't matter, though, because the truth was plain: Erica didn't love me like I loved her.

* * *

It would only become apparent after decades of chasing many such Ericas—and never feeling any better for any extended length of time—that I wouldn't find that for which I searched with anyone else. This was because, truth be told, what I was really seeking was a fundamental sense of adequacy. I didn't feel whole—let alone strong, at the time. It took work for me to accept myself. Had I not done it, however, now, decades later, I might still be seeking validation with chocolate gift boxes.

MANY FORMS

Unworthiness stems from a lack of self-acceptance and self-love. It manifests in a thousand forms, and here are twelve of them. Do any of the following ring true for you?

- You feel empty when you achieve and emptier when you don't.
- You're constantly sick or at odds with your body.
- You're afraid to ask for a raise even though you've proven yourself at work.
- You eat until you're full, and then keep eating to fill the emptiness.
- Your sex life has the turnover and anonymity of an airport bathroom.

- Other people always seem to somehow fail you.
- When someone is in a bad mood or grouchy, you wonder what you might have done to cause it.
- You talk endlessly about your achievements in a compensatory fashion.
- Your bank account has been oscillating between zero and little for as long as you can remember.
- You scold and criticize yourself non-stop.
- You wade through relationships until they dissolve in mutual dissatisfaction.
- You tell yourself you don't deserve anything better.

THE THREE LOVE GRASPS

Over the years I realized we all struggle with self-acceptance to some extent—including the variety of high-flying leaders, entrepreneurs, and athletes whom I've coached. Funnily enough, some people start out convinced that what's wrong with their life is they're not closing enough deals, getting enough done, or meeting enough deadlines. As they discover when we keep digging, however, at the core problem is that they simply feel unworthy. Like they aren't "enough." They'll confess they don't feel good enough, smart enough, funny enough, sexy enough, rich enough, or something of that genre. In almost all cases, I've found there are three substitutes we employ when we don't feel like we're enough:

1. We grasp for others (*connecting*):

We seek from without that which we haven't developed within. It's certainly a valid strategy: who doesn't love being wrapped in someone's arms, lost in their gaze, and told all they've ever wanted to hear? But divorce rates suggest that the experience doesn't last. Soon, it's back to the broken "not enough" monologues. Not to mention, love—as seen in our movies and popularized by culture—is some cocktail of attraction, eroticism, addiction, possessiveness, or control with only a side of legitimate care. While relationships can certainly serve as a tremendous mirror for growth and development, you can only love someone to the extent you love yourself. Sadly, the above strategy, while useful, won't do the trick.

2. We grasp for things (*having*):

I once had a client in New York City who had a high-flying career, was making exceptional money, and only dated models. Often, when the city life would catch up with him, he'd stroll down to the shopping district and buy himself a new jacket. These jackets were not cheap. Before long, his huge closet space was filled, but he kept buying. It was after buying his fortieth jacket that he had a bit of a reckoning, you might say. He realized that his six-digit wardrobe was complete, but he was still not. When we spoke on our first coaching call, I asked him what jacket-buying was giving him. He said they made him feel good, like he was worth something, like he *was someone important*. The problem was that feeling would always wear off a few days later. Then it was back to the "staying-busy" mode to compensate.

I had seen a similar pattern in childhood. Although I didn't grow up rich, I had an older friend who did. She, like my client above, bought things in an attempt to *feel*. Unlike my client above, however, she lived alone in a twelve-bedroom gated estate and had entire rooms in her house that were filled with clothes, most of which were still tagged and unworn. Meanwhile, she still shopped compulsively anytime her schedule permitted.

I remember once she overslept for a Black Friday Sale. She woke up at 8 a.m. but the sales had started at 5 a.m. Frenzied, she jumped out of bed and got in her car before she was fully awake. While exiting her own driveway, she crashed her Lexus into her Bentley, which was parked in her driveway in front of the house. Suffice it to say, the various trips to the mechanic that followed prompted her to look "under the hood" in more ways the one.

3. We grasp at productivity (*doing*):

When people lack self-acceptance, they often peg their personal value to their work. Men are especially prone to falling into this trap. This is because our culture subtly suggests that "being a man" means "proving" your worth in the trenches of your career. The inner lives of men, then, become governed by *competition with others* mixed with the *fear of measuring up*. This plays out across their entire professional lives and drives much of their performance. However, around retirement, men find themselves at a loss for something to do and male mortality rates spike. Retirement effectively means they can no longer get value from their careers and must face the inadequacies from which they have been running for so long. Death is often the preferred option.[45]

---

45 James Hollis, *Under Saturn's Shadow: The Wounding and Healing Of Men (Studies In Jungian Psychology By Jungian Analysts).* (70–75)

COMPETENCY VS ADEQUACY

On one hand, as a species, we're still at odds with nature for our survival. That means part of how we're valued by society is based on how well we can solve problems and get things done. For example, when we solve problems quickly and well, we're rewarded with promotions, status, resources, and other opportunities. I assume this is how "doingness" got tangled with "goodness" in the first place.

But there is a distinction here that we men often miss: competency and basic human adequacy are separate things. Competency is domain-specific. Adequacy is not. For example, I have no competency when it comes to entering burning buildings. On the other hand, a fireman does.

However, I will never be *less* of a person than the fireman because I am unskilled at dealing with a burning building. We are both adequate humans by unchanging birthright.

I mention this because I've noticed a tendency for high performers to propel themselves more by *lack* rather than by love. They think that they'll finally feel *enough* when they reach their goal. Rebels, too, might think "If I do things differently, and go my own way, then I'll finally feel free."

This type of thinking rarely works. For both cohorts—whether ambitious or iconoclastic in their ideals—there is always a point at which an inner lack becomes something of an outer limit or ceiling. From there, the only way forward is to finally begin to do the inner work around self-acceptance.

THE ONLY WAY TO SAVE YOUR SANITY IS TO ACCEPT YOURSELF

My mentor once taught me an effective technique for increasing self-acceptance. This technique came in handy for me while I was training overseas with twenty high-level therapists and coaches.

The trainer was teaching us a new technique and asked if there were any questions. At the time, I was the youngest person in the circle, but this was not unusual for me back then. I raised my hand and so did several others. For some reason, however, I suddenly felt weird. Self-conscious. Uncomfortable. But why?

As I sat there, with my hand still raised, no explanations came to mind. So, I asked myself: *Self, how old do you feel right now?*

"*Eight years old*" was the answer offered by my imagination, which was more than willing to participate.

"Come be with me here in the room," I muttered to myself.

Then I imagined my eight-year-old-self appearing next to me. In my mind, I imagined hugging him and whispering to him: "It's going to be ok. I accept you and no matter what happens, I'll always be with you. You're always enough. You can even stay here with me now, if you want, and be part of this classroom experience."

Of course, as far as anyone else was concerned sitting in the classroom, none of this ever happened. But when the trainer finally called on me, I remember speaking calmly, resolutely, and feeling deeply connected to my inner strength. All of this came from imagining my little guy there by my side.

It might seem a bit unusual to be simulating a chat with yourself for the purpose of self-acceptance, but we're talking to ourselves in our heads all the time anyway, so we might as well get a boost of strength out of it.

* * *

Goethe once said that "The greatest evil that can befall man is that he should come to think ill of himself." It follows then, that the most nurturing act you can do is treat yourself as someone who is deeply cared for. How you choose to do this is highly individual. But remember that there's more to self-care than candles and bubble baths.

If you think about it, life is an ongoing carousel of friendships, romances, and events. Breakthroughs are followed by breakdowns. The only constant throughout it all—is you. It makes sense that prioritizing your relationship with yourself and making it an unconditionally accepting one, will be the gift that keeps on giving. Here are some pointers to help you start the process.

BECOMING YOUR OWN PERSON WILL MAKE YOU STRONGER

REBEL TIPS FOR SELF-LOVE AND ACCEPTANCE

CELEBRATE THE MIRACLES OF YOUR VERY BEING

You are a statistical improbability. Think of your parents meeting each other. They're two people in 7.5 billion. They met at that specific point in time. And then decided to have sex. Whether that's gruesome for you to imagine or not, that means one in roughly one hundred million sperm found and fertilized a well-timed egg. Then, you also survived roughly forty weeks of gestation, "narrowly" made it through to birth, and grew into an adult. I think too much happened for you to get here and spend your life feeling incomplete. The universe has been vying for you, in a weird way. So periodically remind yourself "I'm here for a purpose and I'm enough." Then repeat.

BE YOUR OWN BEST PARENT

If your parents told you that you were loved all your childhood, lucky you. But if they didn't, you best start doing so for yourself today. Start by thinking of the highest compliment someone could pay you. For what do you want to be acknowledged? What would someone have to say (or perhaps do) to let you know you were absolutely accepted? If you have trouble figuring this out yourself, imagine looking at yourself through the eyes of someone who loves you; speak from that place. From this position, what makes you feel love for yourself?

Overwhelm your mind with good things

If the reparenting exercise above didn't work for you, and you don't yet feel especially deserving and want to start, think about what it is that makes you feel love or gratitude in the world. You might imagine pets, good weather, bonfires, pretty people smiling at you, visits from friends, making the sale, a good hair day, the first sip of your favorite drink or anything else, really.

Not everything is a lack of self-acceptance

At a job I once held, a colleague called me a "fuck up" for botching a small project. I certainly messed up, but to be fair, there is a difference between "fucking up" and being a "fuck up;" one speaks to your competency, the other to your personal adequacy. As far as feedback goes, though, I took this as an indication I had to seriously upgrade my skill set before the next project.

This too shall pass

When facing writer's block, author James Patterson, whose books have sold hundreds of millions of copies, reminds himself to keep going, and that he'll just get it on the next round. He then keeps at it. In the same way, when you inevitably experience a lull in your self-acceptance, normalize and validate it. "Oh, look, it's one of those silly mornings again. Not a big deal. Part of the journey. I'll be back to feeling like myself by noon." And then keep moving.

MAKE SELF-ACCEPTANCE AN ONGOING FOCUS

In actuality, the process of self-acceptance never ends. So, plan to make this work a staple of your life if you're interested in inner strength. Consider making your desktop background an image of "you're enough" written on it. I've known people who didn't want to do this because they didn't want others to know that they felt inadequate in any way. If you would prefer to be inconspicuous about it, create your own "trigger" word—something positive only you understand. Put it in another language if you need to, but just be sure to tell yourself: "I am enough. I am always enough." Then repeat this until you feel it and know it to be true. Others will soon know it as well.

"If someone thinks that love and peace is a cliché that must have been left behind in the Sixties, that's his problem. Love and peace are eternal."

— JOHN LENNON

REBEL CASE STUDY:

John Lennon—the legendary singer-songwriter and co-founder of The Beatles—was an iconic counter-culture rebel of the '60s.

During his early years growing up in Liverpool, his reputation was one for trickery and "wasting other pupils' time." School reports deemed him "hopeless" and "on the road to failure." [46] Later, he got into college by the grace of his aunt and headmaster but also got expelled for disruptive behavior.

Some might point to the early painful experiences he had as the latent cause for his behavior: separated parents, an absent father, John being sent to live with his aunt and uncle, etc. His mother, who would visit John regularly, was then killed in a car accident when he was seventeen.

While traumatizing, none of these experiences stopped John from achieving fame and wealth with The Beatles, widely considered to be *the* musical sensation of the time. When he would take the stage to perform, he seemed to radiate confidence and charisma. Audiences around the world responded by selling out his shows with The Beatles and buying millions of copies of their songs globally.[47,48]

---

46 Tejvan Pettinger, "*Biography of John Lennon*."

47 Ibid.

48 "John Lennon Biography."

Behind the scenes, however, John had his own battles with self-acceptance. The highs of commercial success were offset by depressive personal lows. John was once quoted as saying, "Part of me suspects that I'm a loser, and the other part of me thinks I'm God Almighty."

Then when the manager of The Beatles died suddenly from an overdose of sleeping pills in 1967, the news hit John hard. He again found himself adrift—this time, experimenting heavily with LSD, meditation, and the Eastern philosophies. Whether it was related or not, The Beatles split up two years later.[49]

As a solo artist, John shifted his ethos to love and peace. He made a statement to the press in July of 1969, saying, "It was just a gradual development over the years. Last year was 'All You Need Is Love.' This year, it's 'Give Peace a Chance.' Remember love. The only hope for any of us is peace." [50]

At the time, America was waging war in Vietnam. It was no secret that John was against these efforts. In fact, his public anti-war stance nearly got him deported from the US by the Nixon Administration.[51]

But the peace he advocated was more than that existing between nations; his theory of peace ultimately pointed back to the individual person. He urged people to "Think peace, live peace, and breathe peace and you'll get it as soon as you

---

49 Tejvan Pettinger, "*Biography of John Lennon.*"

50 Ibid.

51 "John Lennon."

like." [52] In this case, peace should be applied reflexively—as a way of life, he said. This peace was the kind that could only come from someone who deeply accepted themselves and others.

In an ironic twist of fate, his own life was tragically ended when an obsessed fan shot him dead at age forty. His name, work, and legacy continue to be synonymous with peace and self-acceptance today.

---

52 "John Lennon: The Troubled Beatle."

CHAPTER 9

EVOLVE BEYOND "BUSY"—OWNING TIME

"We cannot start over, but we can begin now, and make a new ending."

— ZIG ZIGLAR

I spent some time living in China in my twenties. When I got there, a friend introduced me to an ex-pat named Bob, who was a senior manager at an American company that has offices in China.

Bob was eager to talk because, simply put, he was nearing burn out. Why? Not for lack of skill. It was immediately evident how competent he was at his work. Instead, Bob claimed his performance was suffering because he wasn't getting enough done, and there was always so much to do. He just couldn't keep up. Knowing that the presenting problem is rarely the real issue, I agreed to take him on as a client.

On our first coaching call, he said, "I feel like I'm in a battle with the clock and always losing. There are never enough hours in the day to get it all done. I need to be on top of my inbox and in communication with my team, but it's non-stop. There are also longer-term, complex projects I need to do, but I'm too distracted at work, so I have to bring it home to get it done. I like my work, I'm just *bad* at managing my time."

As we explored what happened in an average workday for him, he told me a significant portion of his work was "deep thinking" vision and creative work. To produce anything worth its salt, he needed uninterrupted chunks of focus time. However, his open-door visitation policy made this hard to achieve. Plus, a daily stream of endless emails, urgent phone calls, and impromptu meetings meant that Bob spent most of his office hours in reactive, not proactive, mode. It was becoming too much for him.

It was at this point I could have said: *dude, just stop giving your anytime minutes away to anybody, for any reason*—and a large part of his problem would have been solved. But there was a bit more to it than that. (There usually is.)

For example, on the rare evenings Bob made it home to have dinner with his family, he was so tired that even if he got an hour with his young kids, he wasn't present.

Over time, his wife went from being understanding, to annoyed, to intolerant of his mental spaciness. Feeling like he was always a million miles away, whether there or not, she started calling him "an empty shell." That provoked him enough to reach out for help.

IMPORTANT DISTINCTIONS

The first question I typically ask clients regarding their productivity and time management is about alignment: *are you doing the right thing?* I addressed this topic at length in Chapter 5, the chapter on work and meaning.

Assuming that the work my client is doing generally aligns with their values, then I ask them the second question: *are you doing that thing right?*

In other words, are they leveraging their time in a way that efficiently brings results?

Both questions are important and here's why:

If you do the wrong (unaligned) thing in the right (efficient) way, you'll be productive at something you dislike. Congratulations, but that doesn't usually create job satisfaction.

Conversely, if you do the right (aligned) thing in the wrong (inefficient) way—like Bob did —you'll be doing something you enjoy, poorly. That's almost worse. Translation: again, little satisfaction.

Only when you can do the *right thing*, in the *right way* (a well-managed use of your time doing something with which you are aligned) will you be that much closer to "satisfying work" in all the senses. Do any of the following ring true for you?

- You do what's most interesting but not always what's most important.

- You have a hard time delegating.
- You get easily distracted by something in the environment (articles, emails, phone calls).
- You like office banter, so you don't close your office door or put on headphones—nor do you concentrate well.
- You begin working on tasks without thinking about the how or why.

THE SEESO METHOD

I was inspired by David Allen's organizational work to create the SEESO Method.[53] At the time, I needed a useful framework for thinking about productivity and time that accounted for the whole person. If, like Bob, you catch yourself thinking there aren't enough hours in the day to have the life you want, consider applying the following Method to your life too.

The SEESO Method has five components:

1. The Setup
2. Your Energy
3. Your Emotions
4. The Slot
5. The Order

The five basic questions to ask yourself when applying this method to your life are:

---

53 David Allen, *Getting Things Done: The Art of Stress-Free Productivity.* (192–196)

Setup: Do I have the right environment and the right tools to get the task done?

Energy: Am I doing the right work at the right time?

Emotion: Is my mood balanced, and do I have the personal practices to get me there?

Slot: Is this chunk of time sufficient for the task complexity? If not, when would be better?

Ordering: Am I doing the hardest thing first, then the second, third, and so on?

The following is how I implemented the framework into a conversation with Bob regarding his productivity challenges at work:

EV: "So Bob, I understand there's a lot going on at work and you're looking for a change because it's impacting your home life as well."

BOB: "That's correct."

EV: "Great. Let's start by considering your setup. What do you need to do your best work? An office? A conference room? A computer and/or phone? Think about the setup as your ideal physical environment and the necessary tools to get your best work done."

BOB: "I think I just need to close the door to my office. That and maybe silence my phone and disable email notifications for part of the day. That's the only way I'll get any meaningful tasks done while at work, if I don't want to bring them home."

EV: "Ok, a good ol' silencing to get the job done. Agreed. Now, let's think about your energy. Our levels of energy fluctuate throughout the day. What type of energy do you need to get your most important work done? When do you have this energy? For example, I find my best creative work happens in the morning when my mind is fresh and energy is high. I try and plan my meetings and other tasks in the afternoon. I also try and do the hardest task on my list first."

BOB: "That makes sense. It would require me to prioritize my tasks differently, though. I'm groggy in the morning until my second cup of coffee. But I'm no good after 6 or 7 p.m., either."

EV: "Sounds like an ideal time for your high-priority tasks would be right after that second cup of coffee?"

BOB: "That would be around 8 a.m. for me. I've already been at work for an hour then."

EV: "Great. 8 a.m. Now let's consider another rarely discussed aspect, which has to do with emotions. Because—let's be honest—sometimes things come up for us during the workday that get in the way of our productivity. For example, people are generally less productive when they're preoccupied, anxious, or upset. Said differently, if you're caught in a negative loop in your head, it makes it hard to focus. This is where your personal practices become especially important, like meditating or exercising or whatever it is that helps you stay balanced."

BOB: "I'm usually in a good mood. Are there some days where I am in a bad mood or caught up in something, of course… and yes, work is harder on those days, or I don't get as much done. And maybe I don't exercise regularly like I used to. There's no time for that with my busy schedule."

EV: "No, time, eh? Really? I know of many CEOs and Presidents that have an exercise regimen, meditation practice, or both. For example, Obama used to exercise six days a week for forty-five minutes a day.[54] Maybe it's just a question of prioritizing?"

BOB: [silence.]

EV: "We'll circle back to that point. For now, let's think about your relationship with your kids. You said you wanted to be a present father, right?"

BOB: "Yes."

EV: "Then it's about not only making time to sit for dinner but also actually "being there," as in being emotionally available for them, too. Am I understanding correctly?"

BOB: "Yes, that's right."

EV: "Ok, that would mean it's not only about making the time but also it's about how *you are* during that time. True?"

---

54 Kathleen Doheny, "The Obamas: First Couple of Fitness."

BOB: "Yes. And that's right: sometimes my kids speak to me and I don't even hear what they're saying because I'm so wiped out. Other times I'm snappy and have a short fuse. I'm afraid they'll grow up without knowing their dad, or at least remembering his good side..."

EV: "Very understandable. That brings up two more points, which I'll use to indirectly address your point. The first is about how you *slot* your time. The "being there" for your kids can only happen if you create an actual *slot* for it in your calendar. Meaning, if you come home after your kids are asleep, it doesn't really matter how present you are for them because they're going to be dreaming about the dinner they almost had with daddy instead. Slot is the logistical component of your time."

BOB: "I have a busy schedule, but obviously things happen that aren't in the schedule. People need answers to questions. And fast responses to emails. That's what really eats my time and keeps me from getting home."

EV: "Maybe you could plan for those things. As in, create a few slots per day where you deal with miscellaneous/surprise items. You could call them *anytime minutes or anytime meetings*. Those could become the official slots of time you dedicate to others. You'd just have to limit their length to thirty minutes or whatever you saw fit. You can also set 'hard stops' for yourself. As in, you leave, no matter what, at 7 p.m., to be home for dinner with the kids. If getting home is really a priority for you, that is."

BOB: "Hmm."

EV: "Let me tell you about the last part of this method, and you can decide for yourself. It's connected to *order.* Order is about how you prioritize your tasks—first, second, third, etc. Here is the big question to ask yourself about prioritizing: is the task urgent or important? Urgent tasks need to be dealt with immediately and are usually connected to someone else's goals. Important tasks, on the other hand, tend to be longer-term outcomes that are connected to achieving your goals. So, answering an employee's email may seem urgent, but is it important enough to interrupt your critical "visioning" task, most of the time? Maybe not."

BOB: [pause] "Not usually, if I'm being honest. But I've been answering their emails, anyways, all the time and for so long..."

EV: "And it's been killing your schedule. So, if you want your time back, we'll have to make a small shift.

Speaking of emails, another trick is to batch your email responses twice daily. For example, I respond to emails at 10 a.m. and 4 p.m., during windows I've built into my schedule. It's the same idea as anytime minutes, except specifically applied to email. I see technology as there to support and enhance your life, not run it."

The rest of the conversation was assorted pleasantries, accountability structures, and commitment steps, but you get the point: own your time!

EVOLVING BEYOND BUSY WILL MAKE YOU STRONGER

REBEL TIPS FOR OWNING YOUR TIME

Again, there are a million ways to approach the topic and management of time, but how I do it is with the SEESO Method. To recap, here are the five steps to the method.

- Setup: Do I have the right environment and the right tools to get the task done?
- Energy: Am I doing the right work at the right time?
- Emotion: Is my mood balanced, and do I have the personal practices to get me there?
- Slot: Is this chunk of time sufficient for the task complexity? If not, when would be better?
- Ordering: Am I doing the hardest thing first, then the second, third, and so on? Is it urgent, important, both, or neither?

Post-Script:

Bob benefited from adding more structure to his time management. Applying the SEESO Method helped him reduce his take-home workload to almost nothing because he was more concentrated and efficient at work.

It turned out that the day he made himself unavailable to everyone, except by appointment or allotted time slot, no one came to his door. He was befuddled. It was so strange, he later wrote to me. *Out of habit, I kept checking my door, at the slightest sound. Wasn't there someone knocking? I had to relearn what it was to actually do work while on the job.*

What's more, because he made it a priority to be home, he was. While there, he focused on being attentive and present, and the whole family appreciated him for it. As did he.

"The day is always his, who works in it with serenity and great aims."

— RALPH WALDO EMERSON.

REBEL CASE STUDY:

When Cornelius Vanderbilt died in the late 1800s, he left behind a net worth of 100 million dollars. In 1877 money, that was like having around $2.3 billion of today's dollars. How did he end up the richest man in America at the time?

The answer likely dates to his childhood. At twelve years old, his father forced him to quit school and work with him ferrying passengers and cargo between Manhattan and Staten Island. The work sucked, and Vanderbilt hated it.[55]

Even as a child, he was ambitious and intolerant of wasting his time on inefficiencies. What did he do? He committed to doing things better and faster on his own.

It started with him borrowing $100 in loan money from his mother for his own little shipping enterprise. He then learned what his clients wanted and gave it to them: a safe, comfortable, and quick water passage—nothing more, nothing less. As a result, he was able to turn a profit of $1,000 in his first year.[56]

From there, he contracted with the US Government and amassed a small fleet of boats that ferried people between

---

55 Thomas C. Corley, "After Months of Researching Cornelius Vanderbilt, One of the Richest Americans in History, I've Realized His Success Came Down to Just a Few Key Habits."

56 Ibid.

Boston and the Delaware Bay. Soon he was given the nickname "Commodore," which he liked.[57]

It wasn't long before the Commodore jumped into the steamship business. Steamships were all the rage at the time and by aligning with Thomas Gibbons, he earned himself a business partner and a great mentor, too.

When Gibbons died a few years later, Vanderbilt used his shrewd business savvy to force Gibbons' son to buy him out of his share of the business. Experience had taught him that life was short, time was his most precious resource, and that he couldn't waste it living someone else's plan.[58]

Truth be told, this ethos—combined with his hardball dealings—eventually brought Vanderbilt somewhat of a harsh reputation. The elite went as far as to call him *rough* and *uncultured.*

This didn't bother him too much, however. He knew he was a man of little schooling and few words. Plus, he was so focused on creating new businesses he didn't have time to entertain unsolicited criticisms. In the event he was directly challenged for his antics, his emotional composure was so complete that people described him as the calm in the storm.[59]

Over the years, by leveraging his time and energy where it mattered, Vanderbilt became rich—and got to take long

57 "Cornelius Vanderbilt."

58 Ibid.

59 Corley, Business Insider.

vacations every year. At some point, he even purchased a large yacht and took his extended family on a six-month tour of Europe to the cost of half a million dollars, while his ventures continued churning a profit back home.[60]

One of Vanderbilt's grand finales happened at age seventy, when he created a consolidated railway conglomerate. This brought the industry better procedures, quicker shipment times, and even more money for him. [61]

Considering all his wealth, however, Cornelius lived modestly. His biggest interest was living life on his own terms. His lifelong motto, which accompanied him to the grave, was: "Never be a minion, always be an owner."[62]

---

60 "Cornelius Vanderbilt."

61 Ibid.

62 Robert Greene, *The 50th Law.* (46–48)

CHAPTER 10

RELEASE YOUR GRIP—LETTING GO

"The moment of surrender is not when life is over. It's when it begins."

—MARIANNE WILLIAMSON

In certain third-world countries, points out author Gregg Levoy, the locals have a tradition of capturing monkeys. To do so, the locals place a piece of fruit in a gourd and cut a small hole in its side, just big enough for a monkey hand. The problem is, once the monkey inserts a hand into the gourd and grabs the fruit, it makes a fist. Then, when the monkey can't pull its hand out of the trap, the locals catch and eat them.[63]

---

63 Gregg Levoy, *Callings: Finding and Following an Authentic Life.* (10–11)

Normally, monkeys are nimble and used to escaping predators in the wild. They could escape this scenario, too, if they'd just let go of the fruit. But somehow this realization doesn't cross their monkey minds. Instead, because they don't know how to let go, they get trapped; it's ultimately their "grip" on things that does them in. Does this strategy sound familiar—maybe for us, humans, too?

NO GRIP ON REALITY & TOTALLY OUT OF CONTROL

It's astonishing to think that our planet is around 4.5 billion years old.[64] In that time, the Earth's continents have shifted, species have come and gone, civilizations have risen and fallen. If you think about it, the unfolding of things has barely anything to do with us: little acorns become trees, cells fertilize into a beautiful baby, gravity keeps stuff from floating off into space.

Yet, a good portion of our lives is spent trying to make things the way we want them, instead of letting them unfold according to those same forces that organize our universe. In this regard, the cosmos doesn't care: the flow of life didn't start when we were born, nor will it stop once we're gone. But we try to control it anyway. Like the little monkeys, we tug at the thing we want and if we get it, we don't want to let go. Then the battle between our individual wills and the flow of life becomes an oppositional one.

Do any of these ring true for you?

---

64 Nola Redd, "How Old Is Earth?"

- You spend inordinate amounts of time trying to prevent bad things from happening.
- Even when you know you're not in control of the situation, you can't let go. Backseat driver, anyone?
- You take personal failures hard; after all, you should have done better.
- You believe that only you control the outcome of any given situation, without acknowledging other possible influences, obstacles, or biases.
- You're caught up in the past and often miss the present.
- You don't feel right asking for help, so you do as much as you can yourself.
- You wish other people were different. Especially your family.
- You prefer to have the last say because you know best.
- You've been called a control freak more than once.

THE ILLUSORY UPSIDE OF CONTROL

Control is mostly an illusion, albeit a persistent one. It's designed to keep us feeling safe despite the unnerving ambiguity of life. This uncertainty, however, is part of the ongoing melodrama from which no human can escape. It's a fact: for every problem we solve, another will just appear. Our challenges will never end, and there will always be unknowns. Such is life. Internalizing this on a deep level makes something like control seem effortful and redundant.

That's not to say we should sit idly and let our bills go unpaid and our minds soften while we regress back to primate form. Life wants our participation, not for us to stand on the sidelines and watch. The distinction here is learning to balance our being in the world with our impulse to manage it.

THE STOIC ARCHER

As early as the 3rd century BC, the Stoics developed a relevant analogy for letting go that pertains to the archer. The archer has a bow, an arrow, and a target. Moreover, he has his expert training and the accuracy of his aim: those things he can control. Everything else—the wind, any obstacles that might get in the way, even the target itself—can't be controlled. So, really all the archer can do is be prepared, show up, put the arrow on the bow and pull back. Once the archer releases, the rest is up to nature.

Translated for modern application:

- You can be the best teacher, but you can't make people learn.
- You can throw the world's best event, but you can't control who shows up.
- You can have the tightest sales pitch, but you can't guarantee your prospects buy.
- You can clarify your points, but you can't make people understand.
- You can be the best leader, but you can't control whether people follow you.
- You can manage your company, but you can't control the competition.
- Or in my line of work: you could be a great coach, but you can't make a client implement your advice.

This is to say that a balanced relationship with control comes from learning to distinguish between what is under your control and what is not. What falls within your sphere of influence? Knowing this, we stop wasting time and energy on things that don't matter and attune to the things that do—things that move the needle. Perhaps we even plan for uncertainty by entertaining more abstract concepts like luck, destiny, and fate, as our ancestors used to.

The paradox is, by relinquishing control and learning to more fully surrender, our lives get noticeably better. Interpersonal conflicts begin to ebb. Performance improves. Self-sabotage starts to vanish. Guilt drops away. As do the shackles of expectation. From there, fear of the future fades. The past becomes mostly irrelevant. The ego-oriented state which connects the two (as in, the past and future) weakens. With fewer encumbrances, our inner strength grows.

This process is not immediate; however, it is progressive. How do you begin? You simply stop believing your thoughts. You start noticing and experiencing what's happening around you. You allow your feelings to come and go with less judging and moralizing. In the thousandth of a second when your normal impulse for control arises, you release.

If you try this strategy for a week straight, you'll likely notice fewer negative emotions, less escapism, more energy, and more presence. You'll start to feel how you're a part of everything and how everything is surprisingly perfect. You'll feel more supported and compassionate and reflect that toward others. Inner strength will begin radiating from your every pore.

Now, the uninitiated may roll their eyes at the last few paragraphs. To them, surrender is still synonymous with enslavement. It still seems like giving up and therefore is antithetical to the rebel.

The truth, however, is that there can be no rebel without surrender. Without surrender, the rebel is someone who swaps one rigid rule set for another. Their actions may ultimately cause shifts in laws, fashions, and governments—but they themselves will remain the same. Without letting go of control, there may be revolution but little evolution—and therefore not more inner strength.

THE OPEN PALM

Take a moment to think of a beautiful butterfly. Have you ever had such a silky, delicate creature land in your palm? While it visits, you can only observe. Even if you're not done with observing its beauty, when a butterfly wants to fly away, clenching your fist—as we humans are well accustomed—will crush the very thing you wish to preserve. I've found this to be like our relationship with control and holding on.

You might find this idea unusual, but what if the purpose of life wasn't about preserving things but rather the opposite: learning to release them? What if we defined ourselves not by what we knew but by our relationship to not-knowing, as did Socrates? ("*I know that I know nothing.*") And if you're not into dusty ancient Greek philosophers, then maybe you prefer the words of author Scott Russell Sanders in *A Private History of Awe*: "We come into this world full of sensation and empty of ideas, and if we live into old age, we eventually depart the same way."[65] As we well know, the tricky thing, for us *grabby* creatures, is what we do with ourselves in the interim.

RELEASING YOUR GRIP WILL MAKE YOU STRONGER

REBEL TIPS FOR SURRENDER AND LETTING GO

MAKE SURRENDER YOUR FOCAL POINT

The founder of the martial art Aikido once said, "I do get off-center, and I correct so fast that no one can see it." [66] When you catch yourself getting frustrated because you didn't get the deal, or the date, or the thing didn't happen as you expected it would, return to your intention of surrender. The same energy you might otherwise use on frustration will become immediately available for finding new solutions. When things get tough, switch the script from "Oh, I guess this can't happen" to "How can I make this happen by surrendering?"

CHOOSE TO VIEW EVERYTHING IN LIFE AS PERFECT

If you keep a journal or list of desires and reflect on what you've written, you'll quickly realize that most of life is NOT getting what you want. For example, I once wanted to be a lawyer—before that a cowboy, and before that a fireman.

65 Scott Russell Sanders, *A Private History Of Awe.*

66 . Wendy Palmer and Janet Crawford, *Leadership Embodiment: How the Way We Sit and Stand Can Change The Way We Think and Speak,* (San Rafael, The Embodiment Foundation, 2013), 95.

And yet I'm none of those things and still happy, most of the time. That's because our brain develops what Dan Gilbert calls *Synthetic Happiness.*[67] Meaning when things don't go our way, our brains shift our perception to be closer to what we actually got, so there's less cognitive dissonance.

Expose your fears

When the impulse to control pops up for you; when you're feeling scared and needing more safety; when any one of your fears emerge; ask yourself: what am I actually scared of? Is it that life will go terribly wrong, or you won't be successful or loved or popular or have money or health? Get to know these fears. Spend some time with them. Ask them what they want. Then decide if the thing you thought you were afraid of is really something you can influence or not. If you can influence it, then it's just a question of "what's the next step?"

Use an open palm

Our efforts to control are often linked with us protecting ourselves against the inherent risk of life, so consider this scenario from self-defense: in a fight, you can strike an attacker with a fist (closed grip) or an open palm. Both strategies will inflict meaningful damage. However, a punch can also inflict significant injury to your knuckles and the many bones of your hand, especially if your fist meets the top of the opponent's skull or other "un-punchable" areas. Striking with an open palm, however, involves almost no risk of finger or knuckle injury and covers greater surface area per strike. A

---

67 Dan Gilbert, *The Surprising Science of Happiness.*

palm may seem like the weaker option, but it can inflict equal damage. What's more, entire fighting styles, like the Israeli *Krav Maga* or the Asian *Silat* use the palm for striking. These are literal examples where a closed grip is not stronger than the openness of a palm.

Acknowledge the Power of Your Resistance

Recognize that you are your number one saboteur. Become clear on how resisting and controlling the various aspects of your life is "stealing from you." Maybe you're limiting new opportunities, maybe you're tiring yourself out, maybe you're just being a drag to be around. Find out for yourself.

Identify at Least Five Surrender Moments per Day

Start to notice and congratulate yourself any time when you come back to surrender status. Operationally, this may be as simple as taking a breath or releasing tension in your body. Or, it might look like this:

- Your flight is delayed and now you're sitting at the airport. You catch up on some work or turn to the person next to you and meet someone new. (A few years ago, I accidentally missed a flight and had to take the next one. While waiting at the airport, I met my future girlfriend.)
- You're stuck in traffic. You can fret that you're going to be late or turn on the radio and have a jam session.
- Got fired? A new job with better hours and friendlier colleagues is out there waiting for you.
- Partner left you? Maybe it's an opportunity to find someone who better suits your long-term needs.

- Car accident? Here's a chance to go on a radically different life path and do all the things that scared you earlier.

CHANGE THE FRAME OF VIEW

Surrender is not about waving a white flag in the face of your dreams and goals. Surrender is liberation; it's the rebel's best ally. It's asking the question, "What am I willing to let go of in order to let my life become all that it can be?" Artists of all sorts ask this of themselves all the time. They also often say their best creations are the ones where they surrender their original idea, get out of the way, and let something bigger take over.

YOU REALLY DON'T KNOW

Admit you really have no idea about the unfolding of things. Be cool with that. As someone once told me, *intelligence* is what happens when you stop trying to be smart.

> *"Easy is right and right is easy. And when you have for-gotten both the easy and the right, you have come home."*
>
> — CHUANG TZU, ANCIENT TAOIST PHILOSOPHER

REBEL CASE STUDY:

Louis Pasteur, the French microbiologist, was born in 1822. Despite starting as an average student, he pushed through years of schooling to earn a doctorate in chemistry in 1847. Louis was the inquisitive type—practical and always looking for ways to solve real problems. In France, a big problem at the time was the spoiling of people's beer and wine due to bacteria. After some investigation, Louis discovered that by boiling and then rapidly cooling the liquids, the bacteria and microorganisms responsible for the souring could be eliminated. His result? Alcohol, vinegar, even milk—stayed drinkable for longer. This was a game-changer for society.

Soon thereafter, Pasteur was asked by the Department of Agriculture to turn his attention to the silk industry, which had been devastated by disease.[68] Pasteur soon developed a method to prevent the contamination of healthy silkworm eggs. His efforts ultimately restored the silk industry in France, Italy, and other countries as well.[69]

By the 1880s, Pasteur had turned his attention to studying chicken cholera, a problem that was threatening the flocks of farmers everywhere. If food or excrement got contaminated with the cholera bacillus, entire flocks could be eliminated in as few as three days. Pasteur eventually isolated the bacillus

---

68 Mary Bagley, "Louis Pasteur: Biography & Quotes."

69 B. Lee Ligon, "Biography: Louis Pasteur: A Controversial Figure in A Debate on Scientific Ethics." (134-141).

and, when injecting it directly into chickens, noticed they would die in less than forty-eight hours.[70] Not exactly the breakthrough result he sought.

By this point, it was the summer of 1881. He had been tied up in numerous projects for as long as he could remember. For this one, it looked like he might not be making headway anytime soon. Not to mention, Paris was stiflingly hot, and he needed a break. So, he put the cultures on the shelf and left for a long vacation. He didn't give up; he just let go.

Months later, when he got back, presumably a bit tanner, he dusted off his cultures and injected the cholera bacilli into the chickens. Strangely, they all stayed healthy. Pasteur assumed the bacilli had lost their virulence and ordered some new cultures. Then he tested them on some new birds and the old ones as well.

The result: all the new ones died, but all the old ones—the chickens that had been inoculated with the other culture—remained healthy.

He suddenly realized what had happened: he had stumbled on a vaccine for cholera. By letting go of the outcome and going on a holiday, Pasteur—the focused, dedicated French scientist—stumbled onto a solution he could have never foreseen. This accidentally led to the creation of two completely new fields of medicine: those of *immunology* and *vaccinology*.[71] By letting go, Pasteur changed the course of medicine forever.

---

70 Ibid.

71 Ibid.

CHAPTER 11

CONCLUSION

"It is worth remembering that the time of greatest gain in terms of wisdom and inner strength is often that of greatest difficulty."

—DALAI LAMA

This is the book I wish I had in my hands when they were trembling with nerves after my various death encounters. Those times were filled with toil and tentativeness, with struggle and search. Such was the price I paid to develop the strength to go my own way.

Now, you've just picked up these ideas for the price of a paperback—so I don't expect you to actually apply anything that you've just read (I hope I'm wrong). It's just that the temptation to stay stuck is usually stronger than the desire for strength itself. Sure, inner strength *sounds* good. But so do money, slogans, status, and celebrity. Hopefully, though, I've helped create a viable alternative to unthinking materialism and thoughtless conformity.

This alternative is not to be confused with irresponsibility or escapism, however. The fact is, being a rebel asks more responsibility of you, not less. Going your own way requires you to become more mindful, not less. How will you be able to color outside the lines if you can't see where they are in the first place?

Also, as you start living a life that is true for you, people will respond in different ways. Some will complain. Most won't. A few will prefer to close their eyes, think happy thoughts, appreciate how special they are, and hope that love will guide them to a miracle.

I'm not ruling this option out, by the way; the love of strength is no substitute for the strength of love. But let's not get too Peter Pan about anything, either. Nothing compares to becoming strong in as many areas of your life as possible because you did the work of wrestling with the hard and ugly.

Expect, however, that some people will go out of their way to stop you. Even now, there are people around whose main aim is to keep us dumb, blind, and silent. History is filled with these personalities, and they've been implicated in Soviet Gulags, Rwandan genocides, and Nazi death camps. These are hurt people, who have hurt others. Regardless of what you've been through or who you've been up until now, you can be different.

To start, choose to stand for something—whatever you believe to be true. A way of life, a cause, a set of values, anything. Dare to share your ideas, your tears, your smile, and most of all, your laughter. The risk of not developing your strength is that you keep all the suffering but get none of the transformation.

Don't worry about doing it all alone, either. Even if the journey to inner strength, by definition, is inward, you will never become strong by yourself. Resiliency has been a community phenomenon since the beginning of time. Anything else is the individualist's illusion (quite prevalent in the West.) So, go on—*do you*—but also share your care with others. It's not impossible for you to be a rebel *and* a team player.

This is the last paragraph of the book. After reading it, you'll eventually put the book down. I hope that when you look up, you start to see examples of strength everywhere because they're all around you. Investigate them. Find and learn from other people—like the models from our Rebel Case Studies—who are healthy, wealthy, and loved—and who already embody the change you seek. Most importantly, remember, this has been a book of advice. Advice, generally speaking, is horseshit. So now forget everything you've learned and go discover strength in the world, for yourself—like a real Rebel would.

APPENDIX

What is Inner strength?

Abraham Lincoln to John Stuart, January 23, 1841, in Roy P. Basler, ed., *The Collected Works of Abraham Lincoln*. New Brunswick: Rutgers University Press, 1953.

Conley, Chip. Emotional Equations: Simple Truths for Creating Happiness + Success. New York: Free Press, 2012.

Greene, Robert. *The 50th Law*. New York: HarperCollins, 2009.

Mansfield, Stephen. Mansfield's Book of Manly Men: An Utterly Invigorating Guide to Being Your Most Masculine Self. Nashville: Nelson Books, 2013.

"PROMETHEUS." n.d. PROMETHEUS - Greek Titan God of Forethought, Creator of Mankind. Accessed January 18, 2020. https://www.theoi.com/Titan/TitanPrometheus.html.

Chapter 1

"Kyle Maynard Makes No Excuses." *Penn State Harrisburg*. July 1, 2015. https://harrisburg.psu.edu/news/kyle-maynard-makes-no-excuses.

Swartz, Bryn. "Heart of a Champion: The Unbelievable Story of Kyle Maynard." *Bleacher Report*. April 10, 2009. https://bleacherreport.com/articles/153858-heart-of-a-champion-the-unbelievable-story-of-kyle-maynard.

Chapter 2

Eisenberger, Naomi, Johanna Jarcho, Matthew Lieberman, and Bruce Naliboff. "An Experimental Study of Shared Sensitivity to Physical Pain and Social Rejection." *Journal of the International Association for the Study of Pain.* (August 2006): https://www.ncbi.nlm.nih.gov/pubmed/16890354.

Greene, Robert. Mastery. New York: Viking. 2012.

Palmer, Wendy, and Janet Crawford. Leadership Embodiment How the Way We Sit and Stand Can Change the Way We Think and Speak. San Rafael: The Embodiment Foundation. 2013.

Sadie, Stanley. "Wolfgang Amadeus Mozart." *Encyclopædia Britannica.* s.v. Encyclopædia Britannica, Inc., Accessed January 23, 2020. http://www.britannica.com/biography/Wolfgang-Amadeus-Mozart.

Chapter 3

Greene, Robert. *Mastery.* New York: Viking. 2012.

Klein, Gary A. The Power of Intuition: How to Use Your Gut Feelings to Make Better Decisions at Work. New York: Doubleday. 2003.

Levoy, Gregg. *Callings: Finding and Following an Authentic Life.* New York: Three Rivers Press. 1997.

Sundem, Garth. *Beyond IQ.* New York: Three Rivers Press. 2014.

Markowsky, George. "Physiology." *Encyclopædia Britannica.* s.v. Encyclopædia Britannica, Inc., June 16, 2017. Accessed January 24, 2020. http://www.britannica.com/science/information-theory/Physiology.

Chapter 4

Albrecht, Karl. "The (Only) 5 Fears We All Share." *Psychology Today*. March 22, 2012. https://www.psychologytoday.com/intl/blog/brainsnacks/201203/the-only-5-fears-we-all-share

"Can I Be Afraid of Phobias? Common or Unique Fears Explained." *Healthline*. Accessed January 23, 2020. https://www.healthline.com/health/list-of-phobias#az-list-of-fears

Greene, Robert. *The 50th Law*. New York: HarperCollins, 2009.

Morson, Gary Saul. "Fyodor Dostoyevsky." *Encyclopædia Britannica Online*. s.v. Encyclopædia Britannica, Inc., Accessed January 12, 2020. http://www.britannica.com/biography/Fyodor-Dostoyevsky.

Chapter 5

Faerman, Justin. "The Eight Keys to Finding Meaningful Work." *Conscious Lifestyle Magazine*. Accessed January 15, 2020. https://www.consciouslifestylemag.com/meaningful-work-the-eight-keys/

Greene, Robert. *Mastery*. New York: Viking. 2012.

"Life Expectancy at Birth, Total (Years) - United States | Data." The World Bank Group. Accessed January 15, 2020. https://data.worldbank.org/indicator/SP.DYN.LE00.IN?locations=US.

Chapter 6

Linden, Paul. Breakfast Essays: Brief Writings on Body Awareness and Life. Columbus: CCMS Publications. 2009.

McCullough, David. *Mornings on Horseback*. New York: Simon and Schuster. 1981.

Palmer, Wendy and Janet Crawford. Leadership Embodiment: How the Way We Sit and Stand Can Change the Way We Think and Speak. San Rafael: The Embodiment Foundation. 2013.

Park, Alice. "Most Americans Spend Way too much Time Sitting Down. Here's How to Avoid Being One of Them." *Time*. November 20, 2018. https://time.com/5459319/americans-sit-too-much

Walsh, Mark. *Embodiment: Moving Beyond Mindfulness*. Unicorn Slayer Press. 2020.

Chapter 7

Andrews, Evans. "When Gandhi's Salt March Rattled British Colonial Rule." *History*. Accessed October 29, 2019. https://www.history.com/news/gandhi-salt-march-india-british-colonial-rule

Cloud, Dr. Henry, and Dr. John Townsend. *Boundaries*. Grand Rapids: Zondervan. 1992.

Gandhi, Mohandas K. *Autobiography: The Story of My Experiments with Truth*. New York. Dover Publications. 1983.

"Mahatma Gandhi." Biography.com. August 20, 2019. https://www.biography.com/activist/mahatma-gandhi

Chapter 8

Hollis, James. Under Saturn's Shadow: The Wounding and Healing of Men (Studies in Jungian Psychology by Jungian Analysts). Toronto: Inner City Press, Inc. 1994.

"John Lennon." *Biography.com*. October 17, 2019. https://www.biography.com/musician/john-lennon

"John Lennon Biography." *TheFamousPeople.com*. October 09, 2018. https://www.thefamouspeople.com/profiles/john-winston-ono-lennon-1931.php

"John Lennon: The Troubled Beatle." *Biographics*. October 19, 2017. https://biographics.org/john-lennon-troubled-beatle

Pettinger, Tejvan. "Biography of John Lennon." *Biography Online*. January 25, 2018. https://www.biographyonline.net/music/john-lennon.html

Chapter 9

Allen, David. Getting Things Done: The Art of Stress-Free Productivity. New York: Penguin Books. 2001.

Corley, Thomas C. "After Months of Researching Cornelius Vanderbilt, One of The Richest Americans In History, I've Realized His Success Came Down to Just A Few Key Habits." *Business Insider.* January 25, 2018. https://www.businessinsider.com/cornelius-vanderbilt-habits-contributed-to-success-2018-1?IR=T

"Cornelius Vanderbilt." *Biography.com.* April 15, 2019. https://www.biography.com/musician/john-lennon

Doheny, Kathleen. "The Obamas: First Couple of Fitness." *WebMD.* Accessed on January 10, 2020. https://www.webmd.com/fitness-exercise/features/the-obamas-first-couple-of-fitness#1

Greene, Robert. *The 50th Law.* New York: HarperCollins, 2009.

Chapter 10

Bagley, Mary. "Louis Pasteur: Biography & Quotes." *Livescience.com.* January 31, 2014. https://www.livescience.com/43007-louis-pasteur.html.

Gilbert, Dan. *The Surprising Science of Happiness.* Podcast. Ted.Com. February 01, 2004. https://www.ted.com/talks/dan_gilbert_the_surprising_science_of_happiness.

Ligon, B. Lee. "Biography: Louis Pasteur: A Controversial Figure in A Debate on Scientific Ethics." *Seminars in Pediatric Infectious Diseases*, Volume 13, Issue 2 (April 2002): Pages 134-141. https://www.sciencedirect.com/science/article/pii/S1045187002500595

Levoy, Gregg. *Callings: Finding and Following an Authentic Life.* New York: Three Rivers Press. 1997.

Redd, Nola. "How Old Is Earth?" *Space.Com.* February 07, 2019. https://www.space.com/24854-how-old-is-earth.html

Palmer, Wendy, and Janet Crawford. Leadership Embodiment How the Way We Sit and Stand Can Change the Way We Think and Speak. San Rafael: The Embodiment Foundation. 2013.
Walsh, Mark. *Embodiment: Moving Beyond Mindfulness.* Unicorn Slayer Press. 2020.

ACKNOWLEDGMENTS

This book connects everything I've ever experienced in my life, so I owe a great deal of thanks to almost everyone.

I'll start with my family: Mom, Baba, and Ruth, I couldn't have done it without your support and love.

Michelle Carhart, for helping me untangle my thoughts and get down to saying something meaningful.

Tony Lillios and Chip Conley, for bringing an awakened artist's touch to business and being.

Thomas Moore and Gregg Levoy: my soulful idols since childhood—what an honor to have your support.

Frank Pucelik, you are the original rebel with plans for the next 200 years and you inspire me to no end.

James Hollis, your work on behalf of humanity is immeasurable. Thank you for supporting the slumbering masculine worldwide.

Lauren Zander, for teaching me about truth and getting purposefully messy.

Wendy Palmer and Avi Grinberg, your wisdom wows me to this day. Deep bow for your help.

Greg Merson: you have the heart of a lion, my man.

Arie Lindenburg: the hero who helped me uncover my hero's journey.

Mark Walsh: for being the sauciest somatic superstar, ever.

Nicholas DiMattina, for your friendship and cooking. Those potatoes, mate, got me to Chapter 10.

The Great Shapov: Enough said. Wowza.

Also, a massive thank you to Eric Koester, Brian Bies, and Linda Berardelli from New Degree Press for the encouragement, support, and advice.

Shout-outs to my campaign supporters including:

Abby Fuqua, Andrew Merheb, Brayton Bushby, Catherine Watt, Chetan Mehta, Chris Lenoci, Dan King, Deron Wright, Dominick Quartuccio, Donovan Arterburn Jr, Eva Zouganeli, Frank Anderson, Gorgios Vasilas, Heigo Juur, Isidore Smart, Jacqueline Foelster, James Nelson, Jeremy Ben-Zev, Jesse Israel, Joachim Persson, Jonathan Davis, Jose Martinez, Laszlo Santha, Leo Ahmad, Leonardo Dal Lago, Martin Georgiev, Max Coyne-Green, Michael Bluestone,

Michael Dash, Natalie Ventimiglia, Ryan Goldstein, Seema Mokhtari, Shane Yeager, Suryoday Basak, Tyrell Ross, and Zahir Surmawala.

I'd also like to thank Aimee, Kelley, Ellie, and Julia for your highly entertaining and totally distracting presence during the Balinese revision process.

Finally, I'd like to recognize my interviewees and friends— both near and far— and anyone else I have yet to mention, for their contributions in bringing this book to life.

Made in the USA
Middletown, DE
17 May 2022